SIZING AND ESTIMATING SOFTWA

CU00836003

THE McGRAW-HILL INTERNATIONAL SERIES IN SOFTWARE ENGINEERING

Consulting Editor

Professor D. Ince
The Open University

Titles in this Series

Further titles in this Series are listed at the back of the book

SIZING AND ESTIMATING SOFTWARE IN PRACTICE
Making MKII Function Points Work

Stephen Treble
Neil Douglas

McGRAW-HILL BOOK COMPANY

London · St Louis · San Francisco · Auckland
Bogotá · Caracas · Lisbon · Madrid · Mexico
Milan · Montreal · New Delhi · Panama · Paris · San Juan
São Paulo · Singapore · Sydney · Tokyo · Toronto

Published by
McGraw-Hill Book Company Europe
Shoppenhangers Road, Maidenhead, Berkshire SL6 2QL, England
Telephone 01628 23432
Fax 01628 770224

British Library Cataloguing in Publication Data

Treble, Stephen
  Sizing and Estimating Software in
  Practice: Making MK II Function Points
  Work. – (International Software
  Engineering Series)
  I. Title II. Douglas, Neil III. Series
  004.12
  ISBN 0-07-707620-6

Library of Congress Cataloging-in-Publication Data

Treble, Stephen
  Sizing and estimating software in practice: making MK II function
  points work/Stephen Treble, Neil Douglas.
     p. cm.
  Includes bibliographical references and index.
  ISBN 0-07-707620-6
  1. Computer software–Quality control. 2. Function point
  analysis. I. Douglas, Neil. II. Title.
  QA76.76.Q35T74   1995
  005.1′4–dc20
                                                            95–6972
                                                              CIP

12345CUP   998765

Typeset by Alden Multimedia Ltd
and printed and bound in Great Britain at the University Press, Cambridge

Printed on permanent paper in compliance with ISO Standard 9706

CONTENTS

FOREWORD

The IT industry has matured considerably in the last few years and is now moving towards a methodical approach that can be described as software engineering. The management of engineering projects, and the environment in which they take place, requires objective information: facts gained from observation and measurement.

Function point analysis is the primary measure for assessing software system size. It is routinely used in performance measurement and estimating, not just within in-house information systems departments, but in contractual situations between businesses and their third-party IS suppliers.

There are standards issued by the International Function Point User Group (IFPUG, covering the Albrecht method) and the United Kingdom Function Point User Group (UFPUG, covering the MKII method). An ISO standard for function point methods is being developed.

Even with these standards in place, evidence from our consulting activities is that there is, in practice, still a lot of misunderstanding of FPA and how to apply it. A major concern seems to be whether the technique is applicable and useful given the development methods used within an organization. Many large IS organizations still have not seen the benefits of adopting these techniques.

This book explains how to measure systems using the MKII method at various stages of systems development and with different types of documentation. It also describes how the size, in conjunction with other metrics, can be used in management – particularly in estimating. The book contains useful arguments as to the advantages that can be accrued by using measurement to aid decision-making. In this it goes a long way to answering the questions of applicability.

As a community, those interested in improving the professionalism of the IS function, so that it can justifiably use the term 'software engineering', still have a lot to do. This book will help. It has been written by experienced practitioners of the method, both members of the Counting Practices Committee of UFPUG.

Charles Symons
Nolan, Norton & Co
1994

ACKNOWLEDGEMENTS

We should like to thank all the people who have helped us in writing this book, including Charles Symons for developing MKII Function Point Analysis and for allowing us to quote from *Software Sizing and Estimating, Mark II Function Point Analysis*, and The UK Function Point User Group Counting Practices Committee for advice on the application of the technique.

We offer particular thanks to Jim McDonald of Standard Life for his role in reviewing drafts and giving constructive and extremely useful criticism.

Finally, we thank our wives and families for putting up with the time we have spent in book writing and for tolerating the FPA-babble into which we have sometimes lapsed.

1

INTRODUCTION

1.1 WHY READ THIS BOOK?

> When you can measure what you are speaking about, and express it in numbers, you know something about it; but when you cannot measure it, when you cannot express it in numbers, your knowledge is of a meagre and unsatisfactory kind. *Lord Kelvin*

> You can't control what you can't measure. *Tom DeMarco*

The above two quotations are only a sample of those that highlight the importance of measurement to project management. Metrics affect all the disciplines that make up the project managers' skill set: they enable the project manager to describe the project, and to make decisions based on objective information rather than gut feeling.

Fenton (1991) defines measurement as 'the process by which numbers or symbols are assigned to attributes of entities in the real world in such a way as to describe them according to clearly defined rules'. There are various aspects of a project that can be measured. Some of these are straightforward to assign numbers to, others are less so.

Project mangers are concerned with information about the performance of their projects. They want to be able to estimate and to track progress in a way that enables them to manage the project for a successful conclusion. Because projects vary in many ways making comparison at a detailed level difficult, information is often required at a summary level and in the form of ratios, e.g.

$$\text{Productivity} = \text{Product size/Effort or cost}$$
$$\text{Delivery} = \text{Product size/Elapsed time}$$

A common component of ratios is *product size*, which is a measure of the relative size of the system under consideration. One way of measuring this is using function point analysis. This book covers how to count function points and explains some of the uses of the function point size.

1.2 WHO SHOULD READ THIS BOOK?

Anyone who is concerned with collecting or using IT metrics (e.g. for process improvement) will find this book useful. Anyone who will be counting function points (e.g. for estimating, tracking progress) using the Charles Symons MKII method will find it invaluable.

1.3 WHAT CAN BE MEASURED AND WHAT IS FPA?

As an example, Table 1.1 is a list of some of the attributes of a project that are candidates for measurement. Not every project would require all of them to be measured and the list is not comprehensive: there may be particular things on particular projects that are not included on the list.

Table 1.1 Project attributes and potential measurements

Attributes	*Measures*
Product	The size of the system being constructed
	The complexity of the system
	The defects discovered
	The changes requested and carried out
Work	The effort expended
	The elapsed time over which the effort is expended
Money	Cost and benefits
People	Skills, knowledge and commitment of project management
	Skills, knowledge and commitment of the technical staff
	Skills, knowledge and commitment of the user staff
Techniques and methods	Management approaches used
	Development approaches used
Environmental factors	Machine characteristics
	Surroundings
	Imposed constraints

This book is primarily concerned with the product size: that is what function point analysis measures. Other metrics are discussed briefly in Chapter 7.

1.4 HISTORY

The measurement of software product size has been recognized as a problem in IT for many years. As outlined above, because product size is a common component of performance figures, it is fundamental to a metrics programme. The difficulties in establishing units for measuring IT product size lie in the fact that IT product is essentially abstract: it is difficult to identify the size of a system. Other engineering disciplines have the advantage that a bridge or a building or a road can be seen and touched: they are (sometimes literally) concrete.

Many attempts have been made at establishing a unit of measure for product size. The more widely known are outlined below.

1.4.1 Source lines of code (SLOC)

This was the first measurement attempted. It has the advantage of being easily recognizable: a source line of code can be printed, seen, and therefore counted. The disadvantages are considerable, however:

- They are language-dependent: a line of assembler is not the same as a line of COBOL.
- They are person-dependent: each programmer has an individual style.
- They reflect what the system is rather than what it does.
- Measuring systems by the number of lines of code is rather like measuring a building by the number of bricks involved in its construction: useful when deciding on the type and number of bricklayers but useless in describing the building as a whole. Buildings are normally described in terms of facilities, the number and size of rooms, and their total area in square feet.

While lines of code have their uses (e.g. in estimating programming time for a program during the build phase of a project), their usefulness is limited for other tasks. If counting lines of code is similar to counting bricks in a building, then what is needed is some way of expressing the system in a way that is analogous to counting the number and size of rooms and their total area in square feet. Enter Alan Albrecht.

1.4.2 Albrecht's function point analysis

Alan Albrecht worked for IBM. He recognized the problem in size measurement in the 1970s, and developed a technique (which he called Function Point Analysis) which appeared to be a solution. Though this was refined (and continues to be refined), the basic concepts remain the same.

The principle of Albrecht's function point analysis is that a system is decomposed into functional units:

- Inputs: information entering the system
- Outputs: information leaving the system
- Enquiries: requests for instant access to information
- Internal logical files: information held within the system
- External interface files: information held by other systems that is used by the system being analysed

Each of these is analysed and assigned an unadjusted function point score, according to its complexity.

General systems characteristics are then analysed to establish an adjustment factor. This is to cater for aspects of the system not concerned with the information handled but the methods used to perform the handling. The total unadjusted function points are multiplied by the VAF (value adjustment factor) to give the function point index (FPI).

The invention of this method was a considerable leap forward. It gives a measure that can be explained to users. It measures the system in terms of its 'information processing mass'.

There are some problems:

- The technique uses terminology that reflects early systems development methods. In particular, until recently, it did not recognize data analysis.
- The measure is not continuous. A maximum size for any component can be reached but not exceeded. This gives problems with large, complex systems.
- It is difficult to measure subsystems and sum the results to give a value for the system as a whole.

In the late 1980s Charles Symons set about resolving these deficiencies.

1.4.3 Charles Symons's MKII function point analysis

Charles Symons's FPA was first published in an article in the IEEE Journal of 1988. A book explaining the technique, its uses and how to calibrate it followed: *Software Sizing and Estimating: MKII Function Point Analysis* was published in 1991 by John Wiley & Sons. At this point the technique entered the public domain.

This book explains how to measure a system using MKII function points at the different points in the development life cycle and, where appropriate, how to convert that measure into a project estimate.

1.5 HOW TO USE THIS BOOK

This book contains the following chapters:

1. Introduction
2. Basic definitions
3. Estimating system size
4. Sizing the system during development
5. Sizing delivered and existing systems
6. Function point counting in systems support
7. Using function points

It can be used on a number of levels:

- General overview
- Reference
- Tutorial

1.5.1 As a general overview

People looking for a broad understanding of function point analysis will find an overview and an explanation of the basic concepts in Chapter 2. In addition, Chapter 7 gives a view of some of the uses (and therefore the implications) of FPA.

1.5.2 As a reference book

Those people who are engaged in a sizing exercise, familiar with FPA principles but lacking practical experience of applying them at one or more stages in the the life cycle, will find guidance in Chapters 3–6. These chapters set out to explain how to apply the technique at the different stages of systems development, bearing in mind the different types of documentation available.

1.5.3 As a tutorial

Chapters 3–7 contain worked examples and each one is followed by an exercise using a case study. This is intended to enable people who have no knowledge of FPA to use the book as a self-tutor. Answers and explanations of the answers to the case study exercises are found at the end of the book.

1.6 SOME COMMON MISCONCEPTIONS ABOUT FPA

As with any technique, there are a number of misconceptions as to what FPA is and how useful it might be. What is frustrating (from the authors' point of view) is that these misconceptions lead to people refusing to profit from the technique. Yet the misconceptions usually arise either due to a lack of practical knowledge about FPA, or as a result of a poor implementation of FPA. Typical comments/complaints that the authors have heard are:

1. *Why waste time in gathering all this information? I know what is required.*
   Often heard from the person who claims to see no need and is often accompanied by 'It takes a long time for no real gain'. There are a lot of people in the IT industry who actually do have a very good knowledge of their own environment, gained over many years. They can estimate and schedule well when dealing with problems with which they are familiar. They normally run into difficulty, though, either when faced with a new set of circumstances or when trying to teach their methods to others.

   This book will not necessarily overcome prejudices. These are often ingrained and built up through fear of having an 'indispensable' position challenged. If, however, the expert can be persuaded that a documented and understood method is preferable to an intuitive approach, then this book explains one such method.

2. *The results are inconsistent.*
   Many people will have had a brush with metrics in the past, but their experience is that they do not work yet. They agree that they see the need, but regard the techniques as trivial or ill thought out. Indeed, there are difficulties when applying FPA, but these normally arise as a result of a poor understanding of the method (often due to inadequate training).

   At present there is no consistent approach to systems development, and therefore a method that can be applied universally 'off the shelf' is not yet available. There are differences in documentation between all environments, even those which profess to use the same methodologies (SSADM for instance). It follows that there need to be local rules: a site counting practices manual. The following chapters, by explaining what needs to be considered at each stage of the life cycle, give guidance to the production of such a manual.

3. *Metrics seen as an ivory tower.*
   There has been an obsession with precision in the metrics world and this may be because much of the work so far has been carried out by academics. Their work is important because it helps us to understand how software development projects behave. However, the application of this knowledge needs a practical understanding that statistical information can only be used within certain bounds.

   There are two distinct groups of people in metrics, the collectors/analysers and the users of the results. Both need to be aware of each other. A metrics initiative can fail if run by a person who regards FPA/measurement as an end in itself rather than a management tool. Similarly, if management has an expectation of absolute precision, it will be disappointed.

   Chapter 7 gives an outline of the implications of starting up a metrics programme and the considerable benefits that can be gained.

4. *That's all very well, but we don't use structured methods and it won't work here.*
   See point 2.

1.7 WHERE ELSE CAN HELP BE FOUND?

In writing this book, the authors have produced a text that will provide help to those involved in applying MKII function point analysis. They both have sufficient experience of providing consultancy to many different clients to be aware that to produce the definitive text that would address every potential problem, given the rate of change of IT, would be a never-ending task. However, they do know that common sense application of the principles documented in this book will allow useful results to be obtained.

In addition, the metrics community (including Alan Albrecht and Charles Symons) recognizes that current methods can be improved. There is soon to be an ISO standard covering function point methods, to ensure that any future developments (MKIII?, MKIV?) will be compatible.

If, after reading this book and trying the technique, further help is required the authors can be contacted via E-Mail:

Neil Douglas at either 100414.771@compuserve.com
or   neil.douglas@pa-consulting.com
Stephen Treble – 100430.1740@compuserve.com '

The Counting Practices Committee of this group is the design authority for the MKII method and offers a 'Help Line' service to members.

2

BASIC DEFINITIONS

2.1 INTRODUCTION

The purpose of this chapter is to establish the need for MKII function point analysis (FPA), and then to detail and explain the basic rules of the technique. By the end of the chapter the reader should understand why FPA is needed, know what the rules are for deriving a function point count, and be able to size a well-structured and clearly documented system using FPA. Later chapters will explain how to size systems when they are not well-structured or when little documentation is available.

2.1.1 Why FPA?

The first question that most people ask about FPA is '*why bother?*'. The answer to that lies in the purpose of FPA, which is to provide a measure of the size of computer systems. If a method exists that allows IT departments to size their computer software, they can then start to derive benefits that previously only more traditional engineering disciplines enjoyed.

2.1.2 How does traditional engineering use measurement?

Traditional engineering typically results in assembly lines producing products; for instance, car stereo system manufacturers produce car stereo systems. The output, in this case car stereo systems, can be quantified in terms of numbers produced and also in terms of the functionality they provide, for instance CD player, cassette tape player etc. By monitoring numbers produced for a given level of functionality over time, manufacturers can plot historical performance rates.

Figure 2.1 shows how, in traditional engineering, raw materials are converted into finished products by the production process. This performance of the process is

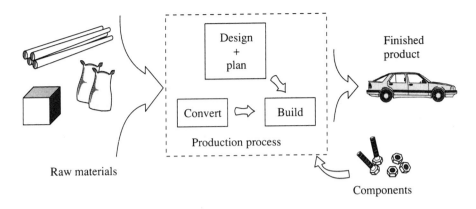

Figure 2.1 The engineering process.

assessed in terms of the quality of the end products as well as the speed and cost of producing them.

When new processes are introduced, manufacturers can measure the gains or losses in performance and therefore assess in a quantified way the benefits (or otherwise) of the new processes. Additionally, when estimating production times and costs for a new contract, historical performance figures can be used to project future performance.

Simply counting units produced would not be sufficient, however. Management information is normally presented in terms of ratios. Typical measures might be:

Unit cost = Total cost/No. output units = Productivity
Amount per week = No. output units/elapsed time = Delivery
Defect rate = No. defective units/No. output units = Quality attribute

2.1.3 Is the discipline relevant to IT?

Until comparatively recently, IT departments lacked consistent measures of product size. This has meant that it has been hard to estimate new work reliably, as well as making it difficult, if not impossible, to measure the benefits arising from the introduction of new working methods, such as CASE tools. Quantifiable figures are essential to management decision-making: the ability to estimate the cost of a project is vital in providing feasibility information, and required IT department sizes can only be predicted by both calculating the size of future workload and by knowing departmental productivity. IT has a poor record in delivering systems that work in the time required and within budget.

In using product measures in the way suggested here, there is a hidden assumption that the process of producing a computer system is defined, and further that it is repeated whenever a new system is built. This assumption bears up when considered; we may have a number of different development methods, even within a given organization, but these methods are repeated every time a new computer system is built, even though the system that is produced may be unlike previous systems in many (or all) respects. In short, like industrial manufacturing processes, the IS development process is defined and thus can be repeated, measured and improved.

Figure 2.2 shows how the process of producing solutions to business operational problems bears a lot of similarities to traditional engineering. The requirements are analysed and defined, a solution is designed and a system produced from raw materials. The raw materials are not as recognizable as in building and civil engineering, but library software, purchased software and bespoke software are the building blocks of a system in the same way as bricks, mortar, wiring etc. are for a house.

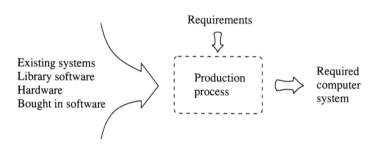

Figure 2.2 The IT production process.

2.1.4 Why use FPA as opposed to other measures?

Previous attempts at establishing size have concentrated on internal measures, e.g. lines of code. One of the problems with these was that they were only an indication of a part of the production process, i.e. programming. There is more to producing a computer system than writing and testing the code. Measuring a computer system in terms of lines of code is analogous to measuring a car stereo by the number of resistors, capacitors and integrated circuits involved in its construction. The number of components is useful in predicting the number of assembly line staff needed, but it doesn't say anything about the functions available in the finished stereo (Fig. 2.3).

What differentiates FPA from previous IS measures is that it does not attempt to measure the product in terms of its components, but rather in terms that are meaningful to the user. To return to the example of the car stereo manufacturer, when dealing with customers the manufacturer talks in terms of functions available (e.g. digital tuning) and not in terms of the components (e.g. integrated circuits). Similarly, FPA deals with the functionality being delivered, and not with the lines of code, source modules, files etc.

Measuring size in this way has the advantage that the size measure is independent of the technology used to deliver the functions. In other words, two identical accounting systems, one written in a 4GL and the other in assembler, would have the same function point count. This makes sense to the user, because the object is to buy an accounting system, not lines of assembler, and it makes sense to the IT

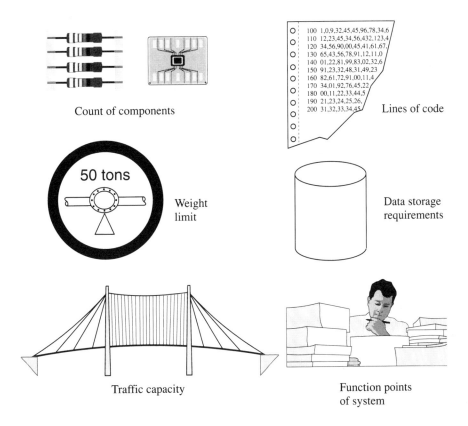

Count of components

Lines of code

50 tons

Weight limit

Data storage requirements

Traffic capacity

Function points of system

Figure 2.3 Hard engineering vs. IT measures.

department, because they can measure the performance differences between the assembler and 4GL environments.

FPA measures the product size by looking at the functionality being provided to the user. In our worked example in later chapters, the system that will be delivered will provide support operations for a car-hire firm, i.e. reserving vehicles, printing customers' bills etc. FPA measures the size of a system by looking at the individual business processes supported by it. An example of such a process would be *print customer bill*. Analysis of this process will produce a number that relates to the functional size of that process. If each process supported by the system is quantified in this way, it is possible to produce an overall size for the entire system.

That overall size of a computer system is known as its *function point index* (FPI). The FPI says nothing about the business value of the functionality: it merely states size. The FPI is a measure of size in the same way that a watt is a measure of the car stereo's amplifier. It is not possible to visualize a watt, but it *is* possible to say that something produces 20 watts of output power; similarly it is not possible to identify something and call it a function point, merely to state that something is 100 function points in size.

It is worth bearing in mind that FPA is of interest because it is *currently* the only measure that works in this way. There will be new function point methods in the future: they may be developed to address weaknesses in the current method (see the section on technical complexity later in this chapter), or they may be developed because technology has moved on and this method of measuring is no longer relevant.

MKII was developed in response to the widespread use of structured methods and therefore sizes systems by making use of the concepts that have arisen from these methods, e.g. data models and data flows. It can be (and is) successfully applied in other environments, such as the object-oriented environment. It may prove, however, to be more natural to produce the function point count in the object environment by examining things such as objects and methods, which are the concepts that have arisen from that environment (and research is proceeding into this). The same would be true for as yet undreamed of future environments.

2.1.5 What does the size measure mean?

Having obtained a size for a computer system, the usual reaction is to ask, 'So what?'. How to use the numbers requires a full book in itself, and we can only partially address the subject in this book (Chapter 7). However, it is useful to make some general points at this stage.

Imagine that a system has been sized at 210 function points and it took 2100 hours of effort and 30 elapsed weeks to produce. We can immediately calculate the productivity as 210/2100 = 0.1 fpts/work hour, and the delivery as 210/30 = 7 fpts/elapsed week.

These figures can be compared with figures for other systems that were built in the same environment and used to assess the relative performance of the IS process for each project that produced those systems (do not forget that measures of quality would need to be taken into account in a real situation). They can also be compared with figures for systems built in other environments, and used to compare the relative merits of working in each environment. This sort of analysis, both within and across environments, is a vital contributor to initiatives such as performance improvement programmes.

We can also say that the 210 function point system is twice the size of a 105 function point system, so we can start to compare relative system sizes and then use that as part of a consideration of things such as defect rates.

Finally, if a new project comes along we can estimate its function point size and use our quantified experience of earlier projects to help estimate effort, duration, headcount and perhaps items such as defect rates etc.

2.2 HOW DOES FPA VIEW IT SYSTEMS?

FPA considers information systems to be composed of two major parts: the information handling portion and the technical implementation. The information handling portion deals with the inputs, the outputs and the processing in-between. The technical implementation deals with the technical constraints surrounding the

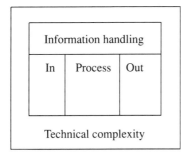

Figure 2.4 The structure of IT systems.

information handling portion. For instance, in the car hire system, a monthly report of outstanding payments is produced. The monthly report is the information handling portion and the technical implementation would be whether it is on-line or batch, whether it was designed for fast response times etc. Figure 2.4 presents this structure diagrammaticaly.

2.3 INFORMATION HANDLING PORTION

The size of the information handling portion of the system is derived by examining the size of each business process supported by the system (FPA calls these *logical transactions*) and then summing the size of these logical transactions across the system being measured.

Charles Symons (1991, p. 23) offers the following definition of a logical transaction: 'A unique input/process/output combination triggered by a unique event of interest to the user, or a need to retrieve information.'

When trying to identify logical transactions, the functions to be performed by the system need to be examined in order to discover:

(a) What the business wants to achieve.
(b) What needs to be done in order to achieve it.

In the example in Fig. 2.5, the business rents a car out and the system must reflect this. To support this operation there may be three transactions:

1. Establish car availability
2. Update cash held
3. Reduce car availability

2.3.1 Key features of the definition of a logical transaction?

The first thing to realize about the definition is that a logical transaction is composed of input, process and output, where the input and output occur across the human–machine boundary. Returning to our car hire system and taking the example of printing the customer's bill, the input would be the details associated with the return

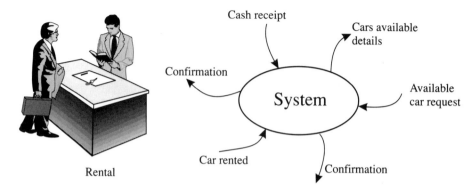

Figure 2.5 Logical transactions.

of a car, the processing would involve recalling customer details, calculating mileage and fuel charges etc., and the output would be a bill.

The second part of the definition is that logical transactions are triggered by events of interest to the user. This principle is extended such that we only size functionality that the user needs and has agreed to. It's hard to believe that IS departments would waste time providing unwanted functionality, but it can happen and when it does it should not be included in the FPA count.

Providing the car hire firm with an unwanted set of screens to store personnel information will score absolutely nothing. Similarly, displaying unwanted information about the customer in the *print customer bill* transaction (for instance date of previous hire) will also score nothing.

2.3.2 What would not be counted as a logical transaction?

If we examine a computer implementation of the *print customer bill* transaction, its possible to imagine a design where recalling customer details may be done by a separate module or subroutine that could be used in many parts of the system. As such, it would have its own input (customer identifier of some description), its own processing (scan customer database and identify candidate customers), and its own output (one or more customers with their details).

However, the operation is internal to the computer system: it is a vehicle for obtaining information that is used for other purposes. The input/process/output does not occur across the human–machine boundary, so this is not a separate logical transaction. It would be part of one or more logical transactions and would be sized as part of them, so therefore we do not need to separately identify it and we would never separately count it.

There is a final qualification for the definition of logical transaction, and that is that a logical transaction leaves a system in a self-consistent state once it has completed. Figure 2.6 shows an example of an 'add customer' screen, where a customer's forename, surname, date of birth and sex could be entered. Assume that the transaction has been designed to be multi-step, with the customer's name being entered and confirmed first, and then the remaining details entered after. However,

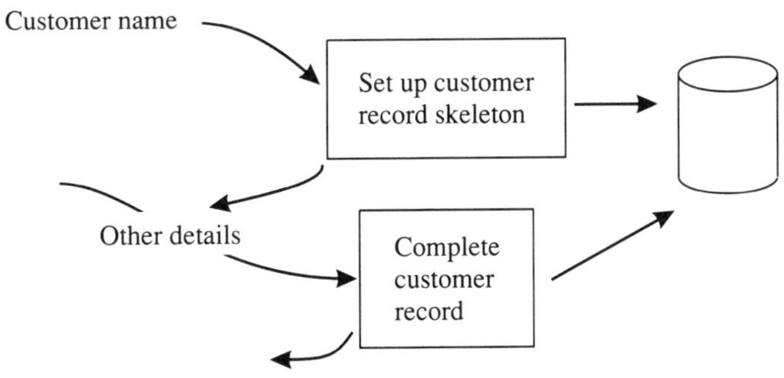

Figure 2.6 Implementation problems.

no customer may exist on the system without all the details being present. Thus, simply supplying the customer's name and then exiting would leave the system in an inconsistent state. In this case, although the transaction is apparently split in two, one cannot be executed without executing the other, so there is only one logical transaction. The logical representation of this situation would not have shown a split, it is a computer design decision.

2.3.3 Where would one expect to find logical transactions identified?

The user requirements are stated in the logical model of the system (Chapter 4 addresses the problems of sizing when there is inadequate documentation; for the purposes of this chapter assume that a logical model is available). Since the user requirements identify the business processes to be supported by the system, logical transactions can be recognized in logical models, either functional (data flow diagrams, function decomposition charts etc.) or data (entity relationship models, entity life histories etc.). The *logical* model is concerned with the information requirements of the system, i.e. *what* is needed. The *physical* model will show how these requirements will be met (with computers, screens, reports etc.).

2.3.4 How do you recognize a logical transaction?

The next question is, how do we identify logical transactions? This subject is covered in more detail in each of the following chapters, since the method of identification depends greatly on where you are in the development life cycle, and also on the quality of documentation available.

However, there are some general points, such as ensuring that you are at the correct level of the business process model. For instance, *Do daily processing* for the car hire firm is far too high a level. *Retrieve car colour* may well be too low a level. There are some general principles that can be followed in identifying logical transactions. Logical transactions can be identified:

- in all cases as the lowest level function of interest to the user;

- for create, delete and some update transactions, as an event (or combination of events) which transfers an entity (or entities) from one state in its (their) life history to another (including creation and deletion);
- for update transactions as events that change one or more attributes of an entity (or entities);
- for enquiry/reporting transactions as events that require the retrieval of one or more attributes of an entity (or entities).

As an example, Fig. 2.7 shows a data flow diagram representation of the logical transaction *availability enquiry* in the car hire system. The data flows *available cars request* and *details of cars available* constitute the input and output. The function *collect details . . .* will be at what is known as functional primitive level (in SSADM and similar structured methods these are known as elementary processes). This transaction satisfies the principles outlined above: namely, it is at the lowest level of interest to the user and it requires the retrieval of one or more attributes of some entities.

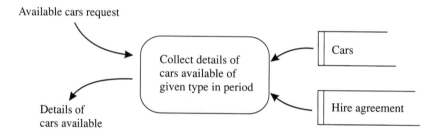

Figure 2.7 The 'availability enquiry' transaction.

2.3.5 How is a logical transaction measured?

Having defined logical transactions in terms of combinations of input, process and output, it would perhaps be sensible to size them in these terms as well. That is exactly how the MKII method works. Thus, to size a logical transaction, we first size the input, the processing and the output, and then combine these sizes to yield the size of the transaction.

The input part of the system is defined as the functionality associated with obtaining information from the user and validating it. The output part is defined as the functionality associated with formatting and presenting to the user the relevant response. The principles of sizing both input and output are, however, the same.

2.3.6 Sizing the input and output of a logical transaction

Returning to the example of the car hire system, Fig. 2.8 depicts the inputs and outputs of the *availability request* transaction, which allows the clerk to identify

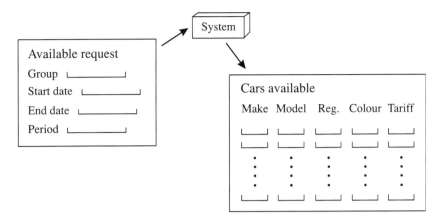

Figure 2.8 The 'availability enquiry' transaction – inputs and outputs.

available cars for rent within a rental group. The clerk has established that the customer wishes a car in a particular rental group, determined by price. The computerized transaction is used to identify which particular vehicles are available for rent given service schedules, rentals in progress etc.

The input to the transaction is *group*, *start date*, and either *end date* or *period*. In FPA we count the number of different *field types*, and in this case there are four. The fact that the user would only use three of them at any one time does not matter: the logical transaction has to cope with four different field types, and the analyst, designer and programmer would all have to take some account of this.

Similarly, it may be that the clerk could enter more than one group (for instance the customer may not care what car is supplied up to a certain group), but even so the count is still 4. In FPA we count the number of different field types, and not the occurrences of those field types.

The output is *car make, car model, car registration number, car colour and tariff*. Clearly, if more than one car was available, a list of cars would appear. However, as noted already we count field types and not occurrences of the field types, so the count here would be 5. Thus the size of the input part of the transaction is 4, and the size of the output part is 5.

Typically input and output fields will relate directly to the attributes of the entities processed by the logical transaction. However, remember that some fields will be derived from combinations of attributes. For instance, the outputs from a logical transaction may be *unit price, quantity* and *cost*, where *cost* has been calculated by the transaction multiplying *unit price* and *quantity* together. In this case, the count would still be 3: the fact that *cost* is derived makes no difference.

2.3.7 Sizing the processing of transactions

Finally, we must consider the processing, i.e. that part of the transaction that manipulates stored information, combines it with input etc. The processing is sized

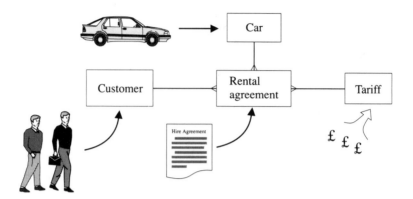

Figure 2.9 An entity relationship diagram. This example shows how the things that concern a car hire system map onto a diagram.

by counting the number of different entities referenced by the transaction. Charles Symons presents his argument for this as a good first-order measure of processing size in his book (Symons, 1991, p. 23). It is beyond the scope of this book to justify the method, but in summary the reasoning is that the amount of processing is proportional to the number of loops and branches, and this in turn should be proportional to the number of data entities handled. Practical experience shows that this method of sizing does provide consistent and reliable results across a wide range of systems and industries.

Figure 2.9 shows part of the entity model in the area used by the *availability enquiry* transaction, and shows how real life things map onto the diagram. The entities accessed by the transaction would be car, *rental agreement* and *tariff*; a count of 3 entities.

2.3.8 Are all entities counted in the same way?

FPA considers the three different types: primary entities, subtypes (sometimes known as subentities) and system entities. Figure 2.9 contained only primary entities; Fig. 2.10 shows parts of a model containing all three types of entities.

Each entity type has slightly different rules for counting. They do, however, share one rule that is similar to the rule relating to counting field types, not occurrences of a field. That is, if any entity is referenced in a logical transaction it is only counted once in that transaction, no matter how many times the transaction may reference it. In summary, the rules are:

- A primary entity is counted once in each transaction that references it.
- Subtypes are counted once in each transaction that references them where the business requires each to be processed differently.
- System entities are counted once in each transaction that references them. However, all system entities are viewed as part of a global system entity, so no

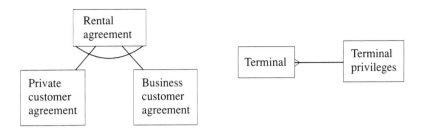

Figure 2.10 An entity relationship diagram showing system entities and subtypes.

matter how many are referenced by a logical transaction no single transaction will ever count more than one for the system entities.

2.3.9 What are primary entities?

Primary entities are the main entities for which the system was constructed to collect and store data. Primary entities are those that the system has to maintain for the user. Examples of primary entities in our case study would be *vehicle* and *rental agreement*.

2.3.10 What are subtypes?

Primary entities may be further identified as entities and subtypes, where subtypes are different versions of an entity. For instance, in this case study, we may model *rental agreement* as an entity but divide it into two subtypes, *business customer agreement* and *private customer agreement*, since each could be processed differently. When counting entities for FPA it is necessary to ask if the business requires each subtype to be processed differently. If the answer is yes, then count one for each subtype; if no, then just count one for the primary entity.

2.3.11 What are system entities?

System entities are entities that are there to support the operation of the system, e.g. parameter tables, code conversion tables, lookup tables etc. Another view is that the system entity contains data that would not be necessary if there were no computer system. In the above example, *terminal* and *terminal privileges* are there to track operations and supply the user with the authorized facilities. If there were no computer, these entities would not exist. If a logical transaction referenced either one, or both, of *terminal* and *terminal privileges* it would score 1 reference to the system entity.

There will normally be a few maintenance transactions on the system, often accessible only by a user with special authority, which are used to maintain the system entities. In these transactions the entities that we are calling system entities would be treated as primary since they are primary to these transactions.

2.4 CALCULATING THE SYSTEM SIZE

Having produced counts of inputs, outputs and entities for all the transactions in the system, it is necessary to turn these into the function point index (FPI). There are two steps in this process. The first is purely mathematical and involves calculating the unadjusted function points (UFP), the second involves the technical complexity adjustment (TCA) and is discussed after we have looked at unadjusted function points.

2.4.1 Unadjusted function points

Calculation of UFP is a straightforward mathematical process once the counts of inputs, outputs and entities have been obtained. The totals for each count are multiplied by an appropriate weight and then summed to give the size of the information handling portion of the system, or UFP. The idea of weights is important, as they adjust for the fact that one unit of input will comprise a different proportion of the system than one unit of processing or one unit of output. This idea is illustrated in Fig. 2.11, which depicts the problem of providing a container to carry a number of vegetables. The container must support the weight. It is not possible to know which would be appropriate – paper bag, carrier bag or box – without knowing the individual weights of the types of vegetable as well as the number to be carried.

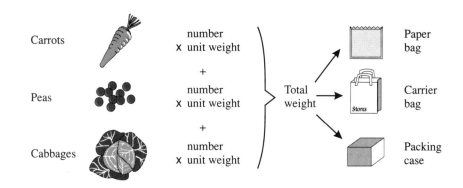

Figure 2.11 Assessing the size of a container for vegetables.

Figure 2.12 shows how the idea of weights applies to the components of a system being sized using FPA.

The industry standard weights used in FPA currently recommended by the UK Function Point User Group Counting Practices Committee are those originally developed by Nolan Norton and Company in 1988 and revisited in 1990. The values are:

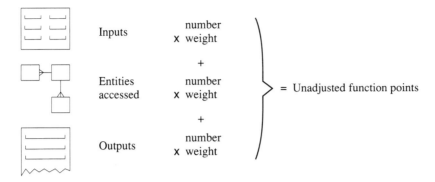

Figure 2.12 The weight of the components of an information system.

Weight of input = 0.58
Weight of processing = 1.66
Weight of output = 0.26

These weights imply that input makes twice the contribution to the system as output, and just under $\frac{1}{3}$ the contribution as processing, i.e. the validation of an input field involves twice the number of logical system components as those required for formatting an output, and $\frac{1}{3}$ the number needed for processing an entity.

The UFP is calculated by the following formula:

$$\text{UFP} = N_i \times W_i + N_e \times W_e + N_o \times W_o$$

where:

N_i = count of the number of input field types
N_e = count of the number of entities
N_o = count of the number of output field types
W_i = weight of input
W_e = weight of processing (entities)
W_o = weight of output

It is possible to calibrate the weights for your own organization. Indeed, it is possible to produce many calibrations, one for each major type of environment in which you build systems. However, each calibration requires that a large number of projects are counted within the environment (and estimates or measurements made of contributions to the system of each size component). That kind of project data is not usually available. Where it has been available, it is the experience of the authors that in practice the industry standard weights will suffice. Greater variations in project performance can be attributed to other factors, such as staffing and technology, than to differences in weights.

If you do produce your own calibrated weights, then it is important to consider when each different set of weights should be used. When comparing projects with other installations, the industry standard weights should be used. When making internal comparisons, the internal standard weights should be used. When estimating, the appropriate environment weights should be used.

2.4.2 Technical complexity

The technical complexity component is defined as 'A system requirement other than those concerned with information content, intrinsic to and affecting the size of the task, but not arising from the project environment'.

The size of the system is calculated as the information processing size multiplied by a technical complexity factor. Figure 2.13 shows how technical complexity affects all areas of processing.

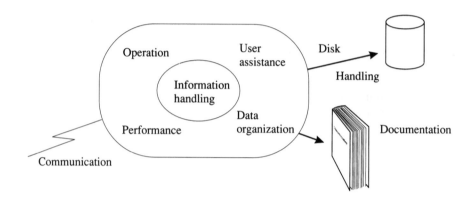

Figure 2.13 The relationship between technical complexity and information handling.

Technical complexity is established by examining 19 factors, assigning 'degrees of influence' to each of them and applying the following formula:

$$\text{TCA} = 0.65 + 0.005 \times \text{(total degrees of influence)}$$

Each factor is scored between 0 and 5 degrees of influence on the following basis:

0   Not present
1   Insignificant
2   Moderate
3   Average
4   Significant
5   Strong

Detailed scoring rules for the technical complexity factor categories can be found in Appendix A.

2.4.3 Calculating the function point index

The function point index (FPI) is equal to the size of the information handling part of the system in unadjusted function points multiplied by the technical complexity adjustment:

$$\text{FPI} = \text{UFP} \times \text{TCA}$$

2.4.4 Technical complexity – the ins and outs

The method for assessing technical complexity is viewed by many practitioners of FPA as one of the weaker areas of the technique. When Charles Symons developed the MKII technique he borrowed the technical complexity idea from Alan Albrecht's original function point method, and increased the number of factors from 14 to the current 19 (or 20 if the site-specific one is defined). The first 14 remain identical to those used in Albrecht's function points.

The major criticisms of technical complexity are threefold:

1. Some of the factors are outdated (for instance TP comms protocols are no longer an issue for those writing on-line transactions). This is one of the reasons that the method of accounting for technical complexity did not change much from Albrecht to Symons. Symons reasoned that technical constraints would diminish over time and eventually cease to be a factor in system size because operating systems and other systems software would provide the technical functionality to developers for free.
2. The scoring of the factors is very subjective, whereas the calculation of unadjusted function points is objective.
3. Where a factor does have an impact, for instance providing a simulator for user training, the impact is usually much larger than the scale of 0 to 5 allows for.

In order to address these concerns, at the time of writing the UK Function Point User Group Counting Practices Committee, the design authority for the MKII method, are examining ways of sponsoring research into an alternative means of calculating the size of the technical component of information systems.

In the meantime, observation shows that the technical complexity in any one installation seldom varies a great deal because the computer equipment and systems software within an installation limits the factors and their degrees of influence. Because of this, a number of metrics groups within various organizations have their own *installation standard* TCA that is used unless the system being measured involves a change in hardware or systems software, or does not follow site standards for development.

2.5 SUMMARY: STEPS IN SIZING A SYSTEM USING FUNCTION POINTS

To perform function point analysis it is important to have documentation that allows identification of all the elements in the system.

Such documentation could include:

* Data flow diagrams with human–machine boundaries identified
* Supporting documentation, e.g. data dictionary
* Entity model
* Access path tables/diagrams
* Entity life history models
* Entity type/process matrix
* Entity process structures

The more of these that are available the better, as they will validate each other, thus ensuring that all transactions etc. are included in the count. It is possible to count with none of the above available, but then the system itself and a person who is clear about the business functionality involved would be required.

As will be seen in later chapters, an *estimate* of system size can be obtained using sketchier information than that suggested above. However, it must be remembered that these are only educated guesses not the result of a measurement exercise. The further through the development life cycle, the more information there will be, and therefore the greater the accuracy of the resulting calculations.

1. *Identify primary entities, subtypes, and system entities*
   Using the rules described above categorize the entities in the data model for the system under consideration.

   In installations where a corporate data model is maintained there may be standard rules for identifying the system entity and subtypes. These definitions might need adjustment, as there will necessarily be systems that maintain the various components of the system entity. In these systems, those entities which are maintained will be primary.

2. *Identify and list the logical transactions*
   This is a very important step: a lack of understanding of what constitutes a logical business transaction can lead to considerable misrepresentation of system size.

   Useful documents for identifying transactions include:

   • Data flow diagrams
   • Process or function decomposition diagrams
   • Create, read, update, delete matrices (CRUDs)

   These documents can be misleading if the analysis that produced them had not been performed completely; ensure that logical business transactions are correct and complete before proceeding.

   It is worthwhile documenting the identified transactions for audit purposes.

3. *Size the components of each transaction*
   Count for each transaction:

Inputs	all input field types from data flow contents, or attributes of entities or relations
Outputs	as inputs, but maintain a separate count
Entities	from data flows to and from logical files, access path tables/diagrams, CRUD matrix

   Note:

   • Primary entities are counted
   • Subtypes are only counted if processed differently
   • The system entity is counted once in any logical transaction
   • For inputs and outputs, count the number of field types, not occurrences of the field type

4. *Sum the inputs, outputs and entities accessed across all transactions*
   Calculate:

   Total inputs   = sum of inputs across all transactions
   Total entities = sum of entities accessed across all transactions
   Total outputs = sum of outputs across all transactions

5. *Calculate the unadjusted function point count*
   Using the totals from step 5 and an appropriate set of weights, calculate the unadjusted function points as:

   $$\text{UFP} = 0.58 \times \text{inputs} + 1.66 \times \text{entities} + 0.26 \times \text{outputs}$$

6. *Calculate the technical complexity adjustment*
   Where an installation standard TCA has been defined, use this if the system is breaking no new ground as far as the IT department is concerned. In all other circumstances calculate the TCA using the rules in Appendix A.

   As there is an element of subjectivity in assigning degrees of influence, it may be desirable to have several independent assessments of the TCA to arrive at the most accurate result.

   $$\text{TCA} = 0.65 + 0.005 \times \text{total degrees of influence}$$

7. *Calculate the function point index*
   Calculate the function point index as

   $$\text{FPI} = \text{UFP} \times \text{TCA}$$

2.6 CONCLUSION

This chapter has defined the basic components of MKII FPA and the general rules on how to apply the technique. It has assumed that a well-structured and documented system is being counted, which has been developed under rigorous project and change control.

Unhappily most systems encountered do not follow the ideal. The following chapters give guidance to applying the method in the more common situations where documentation is either inappropriate, incomplete, or both.

2.7 KEY POINTS

- FPA provides a technology-independent means of measuring the products of the IS process, and hence monitoring the process itself.
- FPA views information systems as comprising two components: the information handling part and the technical implementation.
- Information handling is the sum of logical transactions, each of which is a computer process comprising a unique combination of input, process and output triggered by a unique business event of significance to the user, and which leaves

the system in a self-consistent state on completion. Each logical transaction is sized in terms of the sum of its weighted components.

- The technical implementation is viewed as comprising 19 different factors, each of which is sized separately and then summed to produce an overall size for the technical complexity.
- The function point index is calculated from the product of the information handling size and the technical complexity.

3

ESTIMATING SYSTEM SIZE

3.1 INTRODUCTION

At the start of a project, estimates of duration, cost and resource are required in order to allow project management decisions to be made. At later stages in the project these estimates are revisited, both as more information becomes available and as events occur which affect the project.

MKII FPA is a top-down estimating technique and views the process of producing estimates of duration, cost and resource as having two steps. The first step is to estimate the function point index for the project's product, i.e. the system that is to be built, and the second step is to convert the estimated function point index into estimates of cost, duration and resource. Chapter 7 explains the difference between top-down and bottom-up estimating techniques.

This chapter addresses solely the estimation of size during a feasibility study and requirements definition. Other chapters that contain references to estimating are:

- Chapter 4, which deals with sizing, or estimating size, once a logical design is available, i.e. the next step after requirements definition.
- Chapter 6, which covers the sizing of enhancements, and therefore includes estimating the size.
- Chapter 7, which includes the conversion of the function point index into estimates of cost, duration and resource. This is dealt with separately in Chapter 7 since it applies no matter how the function point index estimate was produced, and therefore is applicable to this chapter, Chapter 4 and Chapter 6.

3.1.1 Why use function point analysis at the start of a project?

The cost, duration and resource required to produce a system is dependent on a number of factors. These can be grouped into two main areas: the size of the proposed system and the environment in which it is to be built.

In Chapter 1, we looked briefly at the possibility of using measures other than function points to calculate system size and saw that other measures had their pitfalls. This is especially true at very early stages in the project, when least information is available. At this stage it can be difficult to identify functionality. Identifying components for other methods, such as how many lines of code will be required, will be more difficult.

Clearly, if it is possible to use FPA early in the project it will provide a measure of system size that can be tracked through the project. This enables estimates to be compared both with each other and with final project actuals, allowing the reasons for variance to be investigated and understood, and hence the estimating method to be improved. It also has the advantage of being expressed in terms that are meaningful to the users since it focuses on business functionality in terms of logical transactions.

This chapter will show that it is possible to use FPA very early in the project's life. The experience of the authors and others is that it does produce useful and worthwhile results. It is worth bearing in mind that because this is a defined and therefore repeatable process it is possible to improve as a result of experience, and thus over time estimating will improve.

As has been mentioned already, at this early stage in the life of the project only the sketchiest of information will be available. Therefore any use of function point analysis at this stage can only produce an *estimate* of system size. Throughout this chapter we shall refer to function point counting, but it is important to bear in mind the fact that the resultant function point index will only ever be an estimate at this stage in the project life.

The second area mentioned above that impacts estimates is that of environment. This covers a variety of topics, such as methodologies and staff skills. These topics are not addressed in this chapter, but are given some consideration in Chapter 7.

3.1.2 What sort of documentation is required in order to use FPA?

Documentation available at the feasibility study stage will be dependent on a number of factors. These factors will include:

- The effort spent on the feasibility study
- Whether or not there is an existing system (manual or automated)
- Project methodology

Quite often the biggest driver in determining the available documentation will be the effort expended on the feasibility study. This will be in turn dependent on factors such as perceived risk, so if the perceived risk is low then little effort will be spent on feasibility and thus less documentation will be available. This of course is not too great a problem: if the risks are low then there is less risk of unforeseen events having an impact on the accuracy of the estimate.

Clearly, the precise nature of the documentation that may be available will vary as outlined above. However, the following are typical for most sites employing structured techniques and one would expect to find at least some of them as a product of a feasibility study:

- Existing system diagrams
- Data flow diagrams at both context and level zero
- High-level data models
- A list of options considered
- A list of preliminary or high-level requirements
- A risk assessment

It does not actually matter what form the available information takes: what is important is that a description of what the user wants the system to do is available at some level, be it at a fairly detailed level or even only at a fairly high level. Clearly, good documentation will become available during the requirements definition; however, before that anything which describes existing systems and lists requirements or options will be useful in identifying system functionality. Similarly, anything describing risks, and to some degree anything listing requirements, will be useful in identifying system technical complexity.

3.2 METHODS OF ESTIMATING SYSTEM SIZE

There are two basic methods of estimating the size of the system: a function-based approach and a data-based approach. Each method requires that the person using it possesses a certain amount of knowledge of the business area under consideration and that they have a reasonable amount of experience in systems development. It should be apparent that if one lacks either knowledge of what is to be built or knowledge of the inherent problems of building systems, then it will be difficult if not impossible to estimate what is to be built. For instance, quantity surveyors will not begin to calculate costs until at least outline plans for the construction are available, and then they would always draw on their own experience to spot implied items that may not exist explicitly on the supplied plan.

3.2.1 Which method is best?

Because of the paucity of information available at this stage in a project it is sensible to use both methods in order to estimate the size. This will help to build confidence in the results of estimating. Indeed, this is generally held to be a sensible approach to any estimating process; the more views of the problem taken, the better the understanding will be and, therefore, the better the resultant estimate.

The fastest (and least accurate) estimate will be obtained from the data approach. This approach, as will be seen later, is heavily formula-based and requires least thought once a data model is available; this is one of the reasons that it is usually least accurate.

As will be seen, there are two different possible approaches to the function-based method, and they both require the function-point analyst to consider the functionality to be delivered. This gives greater opportunity for spotting missing functionality (and even missing entities) than does the formula-based data method. For this reason, and because it is not terribly time-consuming to do (projects of 20 person-years can be estimated in as little as half a day by an experienced analyst), the authors would recommend that the function-based method is always used if time forbids more than one method to be used.

3.3 FUNCTION-BASED APPROACH

The function-based approach views the system in terms of what it is expected to do for the user. Useful preliminary documentation will be a definition of the current system (data flow diagrams etc.) and a list of preliminary or high-level requirements. Essentially, the approach is to try to identify the likely logical transactions and then to size them. There are two approaches to sizing, and these are presented in order of increasing accuracy, i.e. least accurate followed by most accurate.

After explaining each major step of the approach, the car hire front desk system (used to illustrate points made in Chapter 2), will be used to illustrate the approach to estimating the size. At the end of this chapter, a case study is presented for the reader to work through (sample solutions are provided).

3.3.1 Identifying logical business transactions

The first step is to estimate the number of transactions. Input to this step will include the definition of the current system if one exists, the list of preliminary or high-level requirements, and the knowledge and experience of the function-point analyst.

3.3.2 Data flow diagrams

High-level data flow diagrams describing the current system may be available. However, at this level it is unlikely that all input data flows will have corresponding output flows. Also, it is certain that the human–machine system boundary (or human–computer interface as it is sometimes called) will not have been identified. All is not lost, however: for each data flow shown consider the following two questions:

1. *Does each input flow have a corresponding output flow (and vice versa)?*
   If there are corresponding flows, pair them. Beware, because the pair may involve several user–system interactions, and there is every possibility that the pair may not even be related.

   If no corresponding flow can be identified, the flow being considered is almost certainly the input or output part of a logical business transaction and its corresponding flow will have been omitted either due to an oversight or to aid clarity.
2. *Is it likely that the flow would result in one or many logical business transactions?*
   Consideration of the type of data flow will help here. For instance, a flow called *management reports* indicates that there are several enquiry type transactions; estimate what they might be or at least how many of them there might be. Similarly, a flow such as *new client details* could indicate a client file maintenance

function that contains add, amend and delete transactions; again, estimate which ones will be required.

3.3.3 Preliminary requirements

This document may well take the form of a wish list that is a textual (not diagrammatic) list of what the client wants the system to do in the future. It will probably identify functions that will be required. Each of these functions will consist of a number of logical transactions, although they may not be explicitly stated. The function-point analyst will have to use judgement to identify the probable transactions.

A simple example would be 'The system will track debt backlog for those debts outstanding by more than 3 months'. From this, the following list of transactions would be a reasonable start:

- Identify, list and total all debts over 3 months old
- Identify for a particular client all debts over 3 months old
- Identify all debts over a certain value which have been outstanding for more than 3 months

3.3.4 Documenting the transactions

List all of the transactions identified and note against each the justification for their inclusion; this will aid later in the project when the size estimate is revisited and the reasons for variance between the earlier and later estimates are being examined. Having listed them, categorize each transaction as being primarily:

- Create
- Update
- Enquire/report
- Delete

Also classify each one as being either simple, average or complex.

This will prove useful as the project develops and a clearer understanding of the system emerges. Transactions added or removed will cause a change in system size and a consequent re-evaluation of project cost and time-scales. Evidence giving the basis of earlier estimates is invaluable when negotiating possible changes as a result of additional or changed functionality at a later date.

3.3.5 Worked example: creating a list of transactions

Figure 3.1 is a description of the current system at a mythical car hire company called Elbert Super Car. From this, and from Fig. 3.2, which is a statement of additional requirements, we will produce a list of transactions and classify them as outlined above.

The description of the existing system and the statement of additional requirements were used to create a context-level data flow diagram, and this is shown in Fig. 3.3.

A customer enquires about the availability of a car of a particular type. The customer will want to know the price and the terms of hire. If these prove to be acceptable, the customer reserves a car. When the customer collects the car the details are collected at the front desk.

Once the hire period is complete and the customer has returned the car, details of the charges incurred are recorded. If the customer is not an account holder the bill is settled there and then. If the customer is an account holder then the Accounts department is informed, which is responsible for invoice production and debt collection. Only Accounts can specify that a customer is an account holder.

Occasionally a customer reserves a car of a class that is not available. When this happens a car of a superior grade needs to be supplied, though the client will be charged at the same rate as agreed on the original order.

Accounts needs records of monies received etc.

Sometime a customer may walk in off the street to hire a car of any type.

Management is responsible for setting tariffs.

Figure 3.1 Description of the existing system for Elbert Super Car.

Management will want information on car hiring patterns during different parts of the year.

Figure 3.2 Additional requirements for the Elbert Super Car front desk system.

The final piece of preparation is the production of an entity model. This is shown in Fig. 3.4.

The first stage in estimating the function point index is to identify and list the logical transactions. This is done by examining the data flows and making deductions about the transactions based on those flows and the supporting descriptions in Figs 3.1, 3.2, and 3.3. The deductions will of course be open to debate, but at this stage of the project the function-point analyst can only make an educated best guess as to the functionality of the eventual system.

Figure 3.5 shows the reasoning used to produce the list of transactions from the preceding documentation.

Having identified the transactions, the next step is to list them and categorize them. Table 3.1 shows the guide to classifying transactions, produced by Charles Symons (1991, p. 154), which he based on observations of a number of projects across a number of industry sectors. The numbers of inputs, entities and outputs shown are typical for transactions in each category. For example, looking at the guide, a simple enquiry would typically have one input, one entity reference and five outputs. Reference to this guide may help in classifying the transactions.

The final list of classified transactions is given in Table 3.2.

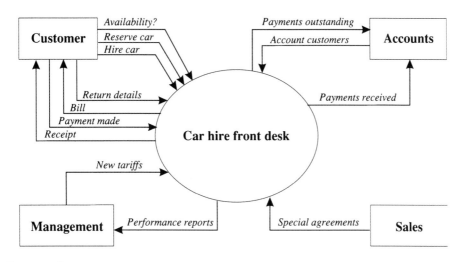

Customer flows
  Availability: Enquiry as to what cars, prices etc. are available
  Reserve car: Reserve type of car at a particular price for a particular period
  Hire car: Hire a particular car at a given price for a given period
  Return details: Length of hire, miles covered etc.
  Bill: Amount customer owes
  Payment made
  Receipt: Produced to prove payment

Accounts
  Payments outstanding: Bills that have not been settled at the front desk
  Account customers: Customers that need not settle at the front desk
  Payments received: Periodic notification of money received and associated hire contracts

Sales
  Special agreements: Special discounts available to particular customers

Management
  New Tariffs: Resetting of prices for different periods, car type etc.
  Performance reports: Reporting on hiring patterns etc.

Figure 3.3 Elbert Super Car context diagram.

Table 3.1 Charles Symons's guide to classifying transactions

	Inputs	Entities	Outputs
Create/update			
Simple	5	1	2
Average	15	3	2
Complex	25	5	2
Enquiry/report			
Simple	1	1	5
Average	3	3	15
Complex	5	5	25
Delete			
Average	3	3	3

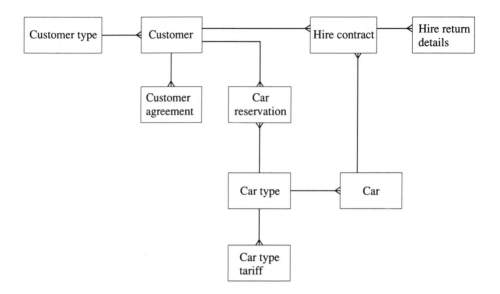

Car: Details of a particular car
Car type: Types and categories of cars hired out
Car type tariff: Changes made for car types during different periods of year etc.
Car reservation: Customer reservation of a car type for a particular period at an agreed rate
Customer: Details of a customer: name, address etc.
Customer agreement: Special terms for particular customers agreed by sales department
Customer type: Type of customer: account, private etc.
Hire contract: Contract made by customer when hiring a particular car
Hire return details: Record of changes incurred

Figure 3.4 Elbert Super Car entity model.

By examining flows to and from customer

Availability   Enquire as to what cars, prices etc are available.
   This is likely to be a straightforward enquiry, with the input of the customer's requirements and output of details of available vehicles.
Reserve car   Reserve type of car at a particular price for a particular period.
   Here the customer is reserving a car at a set price for an agreed period. A *create* type transaction will be required in order to make the reservation. It is probable that there will be a requirement to amend and delete reservations; while estimating, it is worthwhile including all reasonable transactions: users may not fully understand the significance of items that they have not explicitly requested.
Hire car   Hire a particular car at a given price for a given period.
   There are two possibilities here: first that of hiring a car without a prior reservation (customer walks in off the street), and second that of taking up a reserved car. Both of these could be viewed as *create* type transactions, although arguably the second case is an update. In practice, there will be little error by assuming both to be *create*; if anything it will lead us to slightly oversize, which is no bad thing when estimating.

If there is doubt in your mind, then size both ways and see how much difference it makes to the total size.

Again, there may well be an unstated requirement for transactions able to amend and delete hire agreements, although there may be legal problems that need to be taken into consideration. Finally, it is probable that there will be a requirement to look at hire agreements, i.e. an *enquiry* type transaction.

Return details   Length of hire, miles covered etc.

When returning a vehicle, the details of vehicle usage must be input to allow billing to take place. A *create* transaction will be required, together with the ability to enquire on the return details at a later date (for instance to resolve invoice queries) and the ability to amend them.

Bill   Amount customer owes.

Produce a bill for the customer: one reporting transaction.

Payment made   Recording the fact that a payment has been made: one update transaction.

Receipt   Produce a receipt for the customer, a reporting function. This arguably may simply be output from the payment made transaction, but we shall record it as a separate transaction for just now and resolve it later.

By examining flows to and from Accounts

Payments outstanding   Bills that have not been settled at the front desk.

Production of a report giving details of bills that remain unsettled. Accounts will have to send invoices to these customers. Assume that this is report production only and that invoicing will continue to be done manually.

Account customers   Customers that need not settle at the front desk.

Accounts will want to be able to add and remove account customers, probably by changing the customer 'type' between account and non-account. This implies two transactions, one to make a customer 'account' and the other to make them 'non-account'. There is probably also a requirement for an enquiry transaction in order to identify which customers are account customers.

Payments received   Periodic notification of money received and associated hire contracts.

Production of a report giving details, one enquiry type transaction.

By examining flows to and from Sales

Special agreements   Special discounts available to particular customers.

A facility for maintaining these special agreements implies the ability to add, amend and delete them. There is also likely to be a requirement to examine them, i.e. an enquiry transaction.

By examining flows to and from Management

New tariffs   Resetting of prices for different periods, car types etc.

As with special agreements for sales, a facility for maintaining tariffs implies the ability to add, change and remove them, with the ability to examine them.

Performance reports   Reporting on hiring patterns etc.

Vague reporting requirements are one area of systems building that is most often subject to scope creep, as management realize what the system is capable of they ask for more and more. For the estimate we will assume that there are five complex enquiry type transactions.

Figure 3.5 The reasoning used to identify a list of likely transactions for Elbert Super Car.

Table 3.2 Summary list of classified transactions for Elbert Super Car

Transactions	CRUD	Complexity
Customer		
Availability		
Enquiry	E	A
Reserve car		
Enquiry on reservations	E	A
Add reservation	C	A
Amend reservation	U	A
Delete reservation	D	A
Hire car		
Take up reserved car	C	C
Walk in off street	C	A
Enquire on hire agreement	E	A
Alter hire agreement	U	A
Delete hire agreement	D	A
Return details		
Record return details	C	A
Enquire on return details	E	A
Alter return details	U	A
Bill		
Print customer's bill	E	A
Payment made		
Mark bill as paid	U	S
Receipt		
Print customer receipt	E	S
Accounts		
Payments outstanding		
Report on outstanding payments	E	A
Account customers		
Enquire on customer status	E	S
Make customer 'Account' type	C	S
Make customer 'Non-account' type	C	S
Payments received		
Print report of payments received	E	A
Sales		
Special agreements		
Enquire on special agreements	E	A
Add special agreements	C	A
Alter special agreements	U	A
Delete special agreements	D	S
Management		
Tariffs		
Enquire on tariffs	E	A
Add tariffs	C	A
Alter tariffs	U	A
Delete tariffs	D	S
Performance reports		
5 × complex reports (?)	E	C

3.3.6 Reviewing the list of transactions

The final list of transactions should be reviewed to ensure that there are no duplicates and no omissions.

While considering duplicates, ensure that separate transactions are not functionally the same, e.g. 'Enquire on customer' and 'Get customer details'. These are likely to be the same if they are to be supplied for the same user area. If they are being supplied for different user areas, usually recognizable as different external entities at this stage, then they are probably separate transactions.

In order to spot omissions, consider the data that will be needed for this system: it all has to be created, amended, deleted and used. There should be transactions that do all these things, although it is possible that some items of data may never be altered and that some may never be deleted.

3.3.7 Sizing the system in unadjusted function points

There are two principal ways of estimating the system size having identified the transactions, which are detailed below. The methods are presented in increasing order of work required, but also in increasing order of potential accuracy. The more work that is done the greater the degree of confidence in the estimate.

Overall UFP size

The first way of estimating the size relies on average sizes for transactions of a particular category (i.e. create, update, enquire, report and delete) and classification (i.e. simple, average and complex).

From the list created earlier, create a matrix of transaction categories and classifications showing the numbers of each category of transaction by classification. Multiply these counts by the UFP weights shown in Table 3.3 and total the resulting unadjusted function points. Reference to the worked example in the following section should clarify what is required.

Table 3.3 Charles Symons's (1991, p. 154) guide to weighting transactions

	Simple	*Average*	*Complex*
Create/update	4	12	20
Enquire/report	3	10	17
Delete	8	8	8

This table was devised by Charles Symons from observation of a number of projects across various industry sectors. It may be that the table gives better results in some individual organizations or within some specific environments than in others. After a few projects have been sized, a comparison can be made between the estimated size of transactions of a particular category and complexity and their eventual size. This can then be used to refine the above table.

Worked example: calculating size from the UFP table

The summary list of transactions from Table 3.2 has been sorted as outlined in Table 3.3, and Table 3.4 shows the results together with the unadjusted function point count.

Table 3.4 Unadjusted function points working from Charles Symons's standard table

	Simple	Average	Complex
Create/update	3×4 UFPs	10×12 UFPs	1×12 UFPs
Enquire/report	2×3 UFPs	9×10 UFPs	5×17 UFPs
Delete		4×8 UFPs	

Total unadjusted function point count = 357

Estimate counts for transactions

The second (and potentially more accurate) way of estimating the size is: for each transaction identified make a judgement (i.e. estimate) as to the number of fields input, the number of fields output, and the number of entities referenced.

Calculating the estimated unadjusted function points is then a simple matter of following the formula detailed in Chapter 2, i.e. sum each count across the system and calculate unadjusted function points by multiplying each by the appropriate weight and then summing the result.

This method requires better knowledge of the system being assessed. Although it is possible for an individual to do this unaided, experience suggests that it is sometimes better to involve a group of people in estimating the counts.

Worked example: estimating the size of each transaction

From the list of transactions in Table 3.2 and the entity model in Fig. 3.4, each transaction has been examined and counts assigned to the inputs, entities and outputs. The detailed working has not been reproduced here since it could take a book in itself and is still only really an educated guess, but in principle the approach was to ask the following sorts of questions:

- For enquiries: what is the required output, which entities would have to be referenced to obtain it, and what would the user expect to type in order to ensure the appropriate output was displayed?
- For creates and updates: what information will the user want to store, which entities will need to be accessed in order to store this information for validation and update, say, and what response will the user want on completion (i.e. input redisplayed, e.g. for checking, or simple confirmation/failure message)?
- For deletes: what would the user need to type in order to uniquely identify the data to be deleted, what entities require to be accessed, and what response will the user require on completion?

Table 3.5 details the results of those considerations for Elbert Super Car's front desk system.

Table 3.5 Results of estimating the size of each transaction for Elbert Super Car's front desk system

Transactions	Input	Entities	Output
Customer			
Availability			
Enquiry	3	3	10
Reserve car			
Enquiry on reservations	2	2	20
Add reservation	20	3	1
Amend reservation	20	3	1
Delete reservation	2	3	1
Hire car			
Take up reserved car	10	5	1
Walk in off street	20	5	1
Enquire on hire agreement	2	3	20
Alter hire agreement	20	5	1
Delete hire agreement	3	3	1
Return details			
Record return details	10	3	1
Enquire on return details	2	3	10
Alter return details	10	3	1
Bill			
Print customer's bill	1	3	20
Payment made			
Mark bill as paid	2	3	1
Receipt			
Print customer receipt	2	3	4
Accounts			
Payments outstanding			
Report on outstanding payments	1	3	20
Account customers			
Enquire on customer status	1	2	2
Make customer 'Account' type	2	2	1
Make customer 'Non-account' type	2	2	1
Payments received			
Print report of payments received	1	3	5
Sales			
Special agreements			
Enquire on special agreements	2	2	10
Add special agreements	10	2	1
Alter special agreements	10	2	1
Delete special agreements	2	2	1
Management			
Tariffs			
Enquire on tariffs	2	2	10
Add tariffs	10	2	1
Alter tariffs	10	2	1
Delete tariffs	2	2	1
Performance reports			
5 × complex reports (?)	1 (×5)	7 (×5)	15 (×5)
Totals	*189*	*116*	*224*

Calculations
UFP $= 189 \times 0.58 + 116 \times 1.66 + 224 \times 0.26 = 360$

3.4 THE DATA APPROACH

The data approach views the system in terms of the data that it holds, and makes certain assumptions about the relationship between data items and system size. It can only be an approximation. However, for a quick check, given a data model, it will provide an estimate in the same ball park as one produced using the function-based approach.

There are eight steps to the approach, but they can be condensed into two simple steps by rearranging the formulae. The eight steps are presented below in order to show the thinking behind each one, and then the two simplified steps are shown. Finally, a worked example based on Elbert Super Car's front desk system entity model, as shown in Fig. 3.4, is given to illustrate the method.

3.4.1 Full method

1. *Size the components of the model*
From the model, estimate the number of entities, the number of attributes on each entity and the number of relationships between entities (i.e. the number of lines, or relations, connecting entities together). This gives:

$$N_e = \text{Number of entities}$$
$$N_a = \text{Number of attributes}$$
$$N_r = \text{Number of relationships}$$

2. *Estimate the number of transactions*
It is safe to assume that each entity in the system, including non-primary entities, will be created, amended and deleted. It is also likely that there will be at least one enquiry made on each one. Therefore we can assume that there are four transactions for each entity:

$$N_t = \text{Number of transactions}$$
$$= 4 \times N_e$$

3. *Estimate the average number of entities accessed per transaction*
If *average connectivity* (A_c) is defined as 'on average any entity accessed is going to be connected to A_c others' then it can be said that for the average transaction the number of entities accessed will be:

$$N_{et} = \text{Number of entities per transaction}$$
$$= 1 + A_c$$

i.e. the entity on which the transaction is based plus A_c others.

When we calculated N_r earlier, we counted the number of lines (or relationships) connecting entities. However, imagine a system with two entities, A and B. Here we would have a single line connecting A and B, and therefore count $N_r = 1$. The line connecting the two entities actually describes two relationships though, since it describes A's relationship to B and B's relationship to A. So, to calculate average connectivity we need to multiply N_r by 2, thus:

$$A_c = (2 \times N_r)/N_e$$

For our example of two entities, this would give $A_c = (2 \times 1)/2$, or $A_c = 1$. In other words, each entity is on average connected to one other, which is exactly the situation in the example.

4. *Estimate the number of fields per transaction*
It is reasonable to suppose that in any transaction there will be a major entity holding the key information plus other minor entities which will hold subsidiary information. The assumption that we will make in this step is that the number of fields involved in a transaction will approximate to the number of attributes on the major entity plus half of those held on the entities directly connected to it. Therefore:

$$
\begin{aligned}
N_{ft} &= \text{Number of fields per transaction} \\
&= (N_a/N_e) + \{A_c \times [(N_a/N_e)/2]\} \\
&= (N_a/N_e) + \{[(2 \times N_r)/N_e] \times [(N_a/N_e)/2]\} \\
&= (N_a/N_e) + [2 \times (N_r/N_e) \times (N_a/N_e)/2] \\
&= (N_a/N_e) + [(N_r/N_e) \times (N_a/N_e)]
\end{aligned}
$$

The remaining steps are based on the industry standard weights used to calculate unadjusted function points, i.e. input fields are weighted by 0.58, processed entities by 1.66 and output fields by 0.26.

5. *Estimate the size of update and create type transactions*
The first assumption made here is that the largest part of the data flow in an update or create type transaction will be input with a nominal output flow, and therefore the average transaction size for an update or create type transaction can be approximated to:

$$(0.58 \times N_{ft}) + (1.66 \times N_{et}) + (0.26)$$

The second assumption is that half the transactions will be update or create type transactions, and therefore:

$$
\begin{aligned}
\text{SUCT} &= \text{Size of update and create transactions} \\
&= [(0.58 \times N_{ft}) + (1.66 \times N_{et}) + (0.26)] \times (N_t/2)
\end{aligned}
$$

6. *Estimate the size of enquiry transactions*
The first assumption about enquiry type transactions is that they are likely to be mirrors of the update and create type transactions, in that the largest part of the data flow will be output with a nominal input flow, and therefore the average transaction size can be approximated to

$$(0.58) + (1.66 \times N_{et}) + (0.26 \times N_{ft})$$

The second assumption is that a quarter of transactions are enquiry type transactions, and therefore

$$
\begin{aligned}
\text{SET} &= \text{Size of enquiry transactions} \\
&= [(0.58) + (1.66 \times N_{et}) + (0.26 \times N_{ft})] \times (N_t/4)
\end{aligned}
$$

7. *Estimate the size of delete type transactions*

For delete type transactions we can assume that they are likely to be processing-heavy, with nominal input and output data flows. Therefore the average transaction size will be

$$
(0.58) + (1.66 \times N_{et}) + (0.26)
$$

We shall also assume that a quarter of transactions, will be delete type transactions and therefore

$$
\begin{aligned}
\text{SDT} &= \text{Size of delete transactions} \\
&= [(0.58) + (1.66 \times N_{et}) + (0.26)] \times (N_t/4)
\end{aligned}
$$

8. *Total system size in unadjusted function points*

This is given by

$$
\text{UFPs} = \text{SUCT} + \text{SET} + \text{SDT}
$$

3.4.2 Simplified method

The first step of the simplified method is identical to the first step of the full method.

Conversion of steps 2–8 of the full method into the simplified step is a simple mathematical process of combining the relevant portions of the equations in each step, expanding them in terms of N_a, N_r, and N_e, and then simplifying the resultant expressions. The simplified expressions are as follows:

$$
\begin{aligned}
T_{if} &= \text{Total input fields} \\
&= \{2N_a \times [1 + (N_r/N_e)]\} + 2N_e \\
T_{ea} &= \text{Total entities accessed} \\
&= 4N_e + 8N_r \\
T_{of} &= \text{Total output fields} \\
&= \{N_a \times [1 + (N_r/N_e)]\} + 3N_e
\end{aligned}
$$

$$
\text{Unadjusted function points} = T_{if} \times 0.58 + T_{ea} \times 1.66 + T_{of} \times 0.26
$$

3.4.3 Worked example: simplified data-based method

Working from the entity model given in Fig. 3.4, and applying a bit of thought, an estimate of the number of attributes for each entity must be produced. Table 3.6 shows the estimate for Elbert Super Car's front desk. As with the function-based approach there is room for interpretation here, what is important is that the assumptions are documented. Where there is great uncertainty one strategy would be to review the estimated number of attributes with a user or another team member.

Table 3.6 Number of attributes per entity for Elbert Super Car's front desk system

Entity	Attributes
Car	4
Car type	4
Car type tariff	10
Car reservation	10
Customer	10
Customer agreement	7
Customer type	4
Hire contract	10
Hire return details	10

Having identified the attributes per entity, the next step is to calculate the unadjusted function points as described above. Table 3.7 shows the working for Elbert Super Car.

Table 3.7 Calculating the unadjusted function points for Elbert Super Car's front desk system

Number of attributes (N_a) = 69
Number of entities (N_e) = 9
Number of relations (N_r) = 9

$$
\begin{aligned}
\text{Total input fields} &= \{2N_a \times [1 + (N_r/N_e)]\} + 2N_e \\
&= \{2 \times 69 \times [1 + (9/9)]\} + 2 \times 9 \\
&= 294 \\
\text{Total entities accessed} &= 4N_e + 8N_r \\
&= 4 \times 9 + 8 \times 9 \\
&= 108 \\
\text{Total output fields} &= \{N_a \times [1 + (N_r/N_e)]\} + 3N_e \\
&= \{69 \times [1 + (9/9)]\} + 3 \times 9 \\
&= 165 \\
\\
\text{Unadjusted function points} &= 0.58 \times T_{if} + 1.66 \times T_{ea} + 0.26 \times T_{of} \\
&= 0.58 \times 294 + 1.66 \times 108 + 0.26 \times 165 \\
&= 392
\end{aligned}
$$

3.4.4 The data approach: a warning

It must be recognized that the data-based approach will only give ball park figures. However, that is sufficient to indicate whether you are dealing with a 'mouse' or an 'elephant' of a system. One of the authors has used it on a few systems and found it to be reasonably accurate.

3.5 ESTIMATING TECHNICAL COMPLEXITY

As mentioned earlier in the book, a lot of installations will have standard values for TCA. If these do not exist and insufficient information is available to attempt to score TCA, use the following suggested values:

If the system is to be predominantly batch, then

$$TCA = 0.70$$

otherwise

$$TCA = 0.90$$

3.6 CALCULATING THE ESTIMATED COMPUTER SYSTEM SIZE IN FUNCTION POINTS

There is no difference between the formula used when estimating and that offered in Chapter 2, i.e.

$$FPI = UFP \times TCA$$

3.6.1 Worked example: Calculating the function point index

In Table 3.8 the FPI has been calculated assuming the Elbert system to be predominantly on-line. An FPI has been calculated for each of the UFP estimates to show the range of possible sizes.

Table 3.8 Range of FPI for Elbert Super Car's front desk system

FPI based on UFP table	$= 357 \times 0.9$
	$= 321$
FPI based on assessing each transaction	$= 360 \times 0.9$
	$= 324$
FPI based on data approach	$= 392 \times 0.9$
	$= 353$

It is worth remembering that we are *estimating* size, so the figures should be rounded before being quoted. Given the inherent inaccuracies in the approximations and assumptions made while deriving the figures, it is probably fair to round to the nearest 5 or 10 and thus quote the three figures as 320, 325 and 355 function points.

3.7 CONCLUDING THOUGHTS

It cannot be emphasized strongly enough that what is being done at early stages in the project is not measurement, but is, in fact, only an estimate. It is therefore unlikely to be correct when compared with the measurement at the end of the project.

As with any estimating process the output will only be as good as the input and that includes the thought and effort that goes into the process. The greater the effort and care taken in preparing the raw material and the better informed the people who are producing the estimate, the better will be the result. It is worth employing more than one of the approaches laid out above, as this will provide a cross-checking mechanism. If there are large differences in the results, then get another view either with different source material or with a different group of people, or both.

It is important to keep a copy of the material used to produce the estimate, together with the estimate, so that the reasons for variance between estimates and actuals can be investigated. This, together with similar records for other projects, will then allow calibration (and hence improvement) of the estimating technique for the particular organization or environment that the projects are being run in. It is because the FPA estimating process is defined, and hence repeatable, that such improvements are possible.

3.8 KEY POINTS

- FPA provides an estimate of the size of the system to be built. This in turn can be used for estimating project cost, duration and resource.
- A preliminary statement of requirements combined with business knowledge will usually give sufficient information for an FPA size estimate to be produced.
- The technique provides for three different approaches to determining size. The resultant sizes can then be compared in order to increase confidence in the size estimate.

3.9 CASE STUDY

The following case study is presented together with sample solutions in order to allow you to practice the techniques outlined above. The sample solutions are in Appendix B.

In many ways this case study will be much harder to do than would a real-life situation since the only material that you have to work with is presented over the next few pages. You have not had the opportunity to work on the project that produced the documentation, nor is there an opportunity to discuss issues with any users. In short, completing this case study and producing an answer similar to the sample answer will demonstrate a good understanding of the techniques. What is important is not that you arrive at the same answer as the sample answer, but rather that your answer is similar and that you understand where the differences lie.

The sorts of issues that you need to watch out for are omitted functionality, duplicated functionality, decomposition to too low a level, and not decomposing far enough. The definitions of logical transactions given in Chapter 2 should provide a useful reference as you work through the material.

The suggested approach is to become familiar with the material, perhaps by drawing your own entity model or data flow diagram from the text and comparing these with the given diagrams. When you come to produce the answers to the questions, however, please work from the supplied diagrams. The whole exercise should take no more than 2 or 3 hours.

3.9.1 Questions

Estimate the size of the system using:

(a) The function-based method
  - using the UFP table
  - assessing the size of each transaction
(b) The data-based method

Sample solutions are to be found in Appendix B.

3.9.2 System overview

A medical practice covers a number of areas, but its primary function is to provide care to patients. Part of this involves the administration of patient details and contacts. That is the area to be addressed by this system.

When the proposed system is available, the practice will be able to:

1. List a doctor's duties during a particular day.
2. List the patients being contacted on a particular day.

This facility will be for future appointments as well as historical.

The system will support the following areas of the practice administration:

1. *Registration.* Patients will register with the practice. Details such as name, address and date of birth are recorded.
2. *Surgery visits.* Patients will make appointments to see particular doctors at surgery times. On occasions there may be emergency visits that are tacked on to the end of normal surgeries.
3. *Home visits.* Doctors will need to visit patients at their homes. These visits will be booked in advance, though sometimes there will be emergency callouts.
4. *Surgery details.* Details of surgery times and profiles need to be recorded. These will be either regular, e.g. morning, or special, e.g. baby clinic.
5. *Letters.* The practice sends standard letters to patients of particular types to invite them to particular clinics. They also send letters to patients who miss appointments.
6. *Reception.* Reception requires a timetable detailing the day's expected activities and events. They require to report exceptions to the timetable.
7. *Doctors.* Doctors need lists of surgeries and clinics and who is attending them, home visits and who they are calling on. They also must be able to report on their patient contacts.
8. *Reporting.* Performance reporting will be required.

3.9.3 Data flow diagram

Figure 3.6 is a data flow diagram describing at a context level the practice administration system.

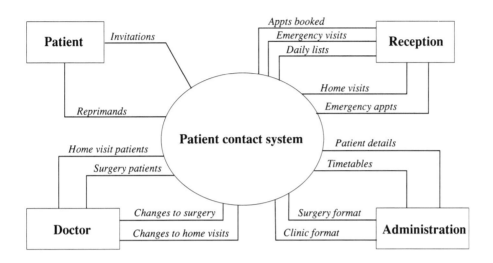

1. *Patient flows*
   Invitations for special clinics sent to patient
   Reprimands for failing to keep appointment sent to patient

2. *Reception flows*
   Appts booked: Additions, changes and deletions to surgery appointments
   Home visits: Additions, changes and deletions to home visit appointments
   Emergency appts: Additions to normal surgery appointments
   Emergency visits: Additions to normal home visit appointments
   Daily lists: Lists of surgeries/clinics and patients for a day

3. *Doctor flows*
   Home visit patients: Details of patients to be visited at home for a date
   Surgery patients: Details of patients visiting a surgery or clinic for a date
   Changes to surgery: Doctor-generated changes to surgery
   Changes to home visits: Doctor-generated changes to home visits

4. *Administration flows*
   Patient details: Additions, changes and deletions to patients
   Clinic format: Details of standard clinics: additions, changes and deletions
   Surgery format: Details of standard surgery: additions, changes and deletions
   Timetables: Maintaining timetables of surgeries and clinics for a day

Figure 3.6 Patient contacts data flow diagram.

3.9.4 Entity model

Figure 3.7 is a first-cut entity model for the proposed practice administration system.

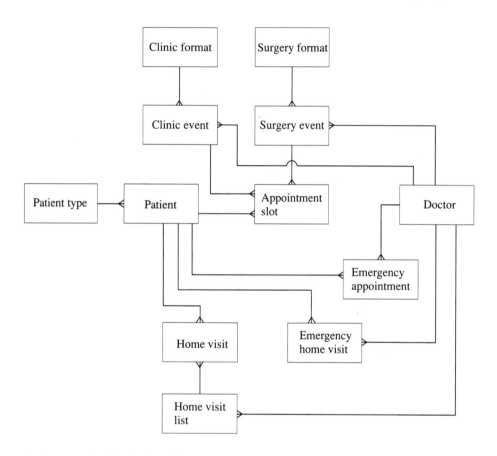

Appointment slot: Booked appointment at a surgery or clinic
Clinic event: An occurrence of a clinic
Clinic format: Standard format for a clinic
Doctor: Medical practitioner
Emergency appointment: Appointment added to normal surgery run
Emergency home visit: An unbooked visit by a doctor to a patient at home
Home visit: A booked visit by a doctor to a patient at home
Home visit list: Booked visits a doctor is to make on a particular day
Patient: Patient details
Patient type: Categorizes patients
Surgery event: Occurrence of a surgery
Surgery format: Standard format for surgery

Figure 3.7 Patient contacts entity model.

4

SIZING THE SYSTEM DURING DEVELOPMENT

4.1 INTRODUCTION

This chapter is concerned with sizing the system during development. The techniques presented are independent of the approach being taken to the system's development and apply at any point in the development life cycle.

4.1.1 Why measure the system during development?

The system needs to be measured during development for two major reasons:

- To verify/adjust previous size estimates for project progress assessment
- To develop estimates for the rest of the project

As a project progresses, the *project actuals*, expressed in terms of effort and time-scales, are used to assess the progress of the project against the project plan. For most projects there will be some deviation from the plan. The reasons for deviation are varied, but can typically be categorized as:

- The *project* is not performing as expected
- The *product* is a different size

Revisiting the size of the system during development allows project managers to quantify the revised product size and to estimate the project performance. This quantified knowledge can then be fed into the planning process and remedial action identified and taken as necessary.

These figures of system size together with the estimated project performance figures can be used to re-estimate the remainder of the project. The re-estimate can then be used for normal project management decisions, e.g. assessment of project viability or development of project plans.

4.1.2 Documentation for recording function point counts

Documentation used for recording counts at this stage is no different from counting at any other stage in the project life. A sample worksheet is shown in Fig. 4.1.

It should be possible to cross refer between the documentation used to identify the transactions and those documents used to identify input and output. For instance, if an event/entity cross-reference matrix is used to identify transactions and DFDs are used to identify input and output, then indicate the events on the DFD (a useful exercise regardless of whether FPA is being carried out). Figure 4.2 shows an example of how this can be done.

4.2 POTENTIAL SOURCE DOCUMENTATION

Clearly some representation of the system is required in order to calculate the size. At the end of the project there will be a completed system that can, if necessary, be used as a reference point for sizing. During the project, however, it is necessary to

---

Transaction counting worksheet

SYSTEM: *Car Hire*
SYSTEM AREA: *Reservations*

Transaction	Input	Entities	Output
1. Make a reservation	New reservation instruction	Car type Tariff Reservation Customer Account customer Customer agreement	Reservation made Reservation not possible
2. Obtain reservation details for a change	Get old reservation	Car type Reservation Customer	Old reservation
3. Change a reservation	Change reservation	Car type Tariff Reservation Customer Account customer Customer agreement	Change made Change not possible
4. Delete a reservation	Car not required	Car type Reservation Customer User User type User privileges	Reservation cancelled Cancellation not possible

Figure 4.1 Sample worksheet for recording function point counts.

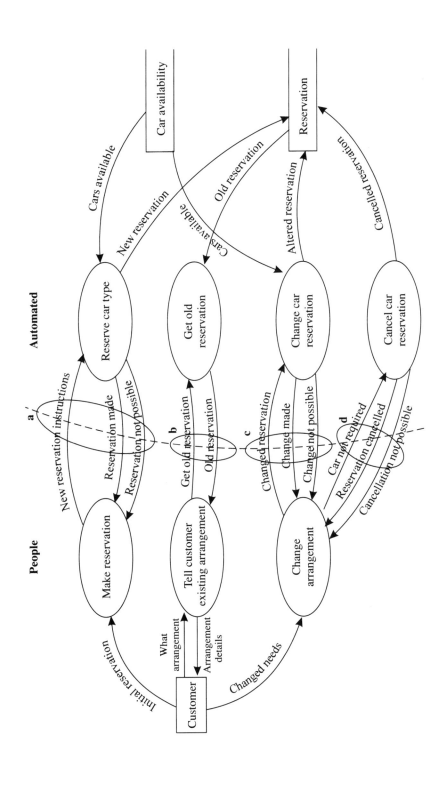

Figure 4.2 An example of marking logical transactions on a DFD with the events that trigger them.

rely on the documentation produced as a result of the development methodology, techniques and/or tools used.

4.2.1 Which methodology, techniques and/or tools must be used?

The most commonly stated reasons for project teams not using FPA are that 'The methodology does not allow us to measure the system', 'We don't produce data flow diagrams' or 'We don't do data analysis'. However, consider the generic model of systems development in Fig. 4.3. On examination it will become clear that documentation sufficient to allow measurement will be produced no matter which actual methodology, technique or tool is used, subject of course to it being used correctly.

Any project will comprise two major phases: *analysis* and *synthesis*. During *analysis*, research is done in order to identify, define and scope the problem that must be solved. This process of analysis results in a statement of requirements (which may be expressed in a number of ways, e.g. diagrams, text, sample system) that simply describes the features that would be required of a solution in order to solve the problem satisfactorily.

During *synthesis* a solution is designed, built and implemented. It is normal for the implemented solution then to be tested against the agreed requirements in order to ensure that the problem has been solved satisfactorily.

Figure 4.3 shows how these two major phases are broken down into software development steps. This is a generic model: most (if not all) methodologies will have stages/phases (or whatever they choose to call them) that fall into or encompass the steps shown. While the generic model depicts a 'waterfall' approach, the two phases of analysis and synthesis are to be found in other approaches, e.g. prototyping.

It is during *detailed analysis* that the problem is decomposed into its constituent parts; this is the process that results in the requirements of the proposed system being documented in such a way that the user can understand them, thus ensuring that the proposed system will do all that is required in order to solve the original problem.

These requirements also need to be understood by the designers so that they can produce a systems model that encompasses them all – the *logical design*. This is the

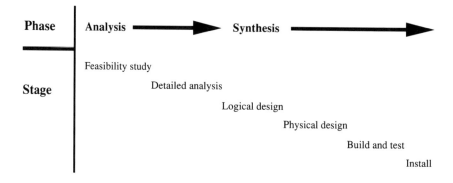

Figure 4.3 A generic model of systems development.

model, in whatever form it is presented, that will be used to calculate the unadjusted function points (UFP). In SSADM this would be documented in the required systems data flow model, the requirements catalogue and the logical data model produced during stages 2 and 3.

The logical design will specify:

- What information will be supplied by who and for what purpose
- What information will be required by who and for what purpose
- What information needs to be held in the system
- The events that cause storage, amendment or retrieval of information

There will be other user requirements, supplementary to the information handling aspect, which will detail more technical aspects of the system, e.g. how frequently the information is required, how quickly the system needs to respond and how helpful/ usable the system will need to be. These aspects, however they are expressed, will provide the material for calculating the technical complexity adjustment. In SSADM they would be known as non-functional requirements and be found in the requirements catalogue.

Before logical design there is insufficient detail to measure the system size, and it is only possible therefore to estimate size prior to completion of the logical design.

In subsequent phases the component parts of the design will be combined/split to enable the system to be built within the available environment (e.g. the function model in SSADM), and thus the models produced in these phases may make it harder to size the logical functionality. The logical design, or whatever it may be called in different methodologies, is therefore the most suitable vehicle for sizing systems and is the subject of this chapter.

4.2.2 What are the features of a logical design?

As we have seen, a logical design describes the information handling part of a system; this can be viewed in two dimensions: function and data.

The *functional view* will show how information is being processed, i.e. what is happening to it. This may be reflected in:

- Data flow diagrams
- Functional hierarchies

The *data view* will show how the data of interest to the system is structured, and the events that either cause changes to the data or that cause the system to supply information. These may be encompassed in:

- Entity relationship models
- Event/entity matrices

Subsidiary documents should be available that support the above, e.g.

- Data dictionary descriptions of the components of both the data flow diagrams and the functional hierarchies
- Entity descriptions

- Entity life history models
- Entity access paths

In addition there may be documents that provide a cross-reference between the two views:

- Entity/datastore cross-references
- Event/process cross-references
- Entity/process models

Whichever form the documentation takes, the language that is used should be free from references to how the system will be physically implemented on the computer, although the boundary of automation should be apparent (i.e. it should be possible to tell what will be implemented on the computer system, but not how it will be done).

4.3 IDENTIFYING MKII FUNCTION POINT ANALYSIS COMPONENTS

This is straightforward using *logical design* documents. If a complete, user-accepted logical design that has been decomposed to the correct level is available, then function point analysis is simple. In fact, if the documentation is held in a CASE tool, the whole process can be automated.

Unfortunately, real life is not that simple. There are projects where the logical design documentation may be:

- not complete
- not accepted by the customer
- not decomposed to the correct level
- not actually a logical design
- non-existent

Sadly these situations are not uncommon and these are therefore addressed throughout the chapter. There is, however, a disturbing question that is raised by these projects (although further consideration of the question and the implications of its answer are outside the scope of this book), and that is 'if a project team has not defined and modelled the requirements of a system in such a way that the user can understand them, then how do the team know what to build into the system and how do they know that the resultant system is fit for its purpose?'.

4.3.1 What approach should be taken to identify logical transactions?

There are in general two approaches that can be taken: first to examine the diagrams representing the functional view and second to examine those representing the data view. Both approaches will give the same answer if the underlying documents depict the same system (i.e. if they correlate), and personal taste will dictate which approach to take. It may well be better to use both.

Where documentation is inadequate, the person attempting to count must fall back on his or her own analysis skills and work with a project team member in order to identify the components. In this case experience shows that the techniques described for the two approaches still apply; however, both approaches must be used and often entity models will have to be constructed. Many of the principles described in Chapter 5 must also be applied. In short it makes function point counting harder, but by no means impossible.

4.3.2 The functional approach

The documents normally available for this approach are data flow diagrams and function decomposition models. Where these are not available, or inadequate, then a top-down approach should be used to decompose the system into logical transactions. This must be done hand in hand with building an entity model and charting information flows.

It will be shown in this section that, of the two types of diagram, data flow diagrams are preferred and that it is difficult, if not impossible, to size from function decomposition models.

4.3.3 Data flow diagrams

When examining data flow diagrams it is important to identify the correct level. This should normally be the bottom level: some methodologies call items depicted at this level *functional primitives* or *elementary processes*. The correct level can be identified by the fact that it documents the base functions performed by the system and that each process is triggered by a unique business event.

It is worth noting that a problem many methodologies have with the use of data flow diagrams is defining when to stop expanding down to the next level. For function point analysis it is imperative that the correct level is used to count the system size. Using the identification of logical transactions as the criterion for determining which is the lowest level of expansion seems to fit with most methodologies and assists with function point counting.

At the logical transaction level the user will recognize discrete interactions with the system which perform viable business operations, i.e. those that amend business information held by the system or supply business information to make a business decision. These interactions (which the user would recognize) are in effect what we term logical transactions. Thus, to identify logical transactions look for interactions: these can be found by looking for data flows into the system and consequent flows out, i.e. triggers and responses.

It may be necessary to refer to the data dictionary to establish what the system functions are actually doing, but, if the function point counter has sufficient business or system knowledge, it may well be obvious from the diagrams themselves.

When considering data flow diagrams, the flows that need examination are those that cross the boundary between the *people* part (the part that will remain manual) and the *automated* part (the part that will become the computer system).

Figure 4.4 shows how the car reservations system deals with customers making and changing reservations. The *people* part of the system specifies how the clerk

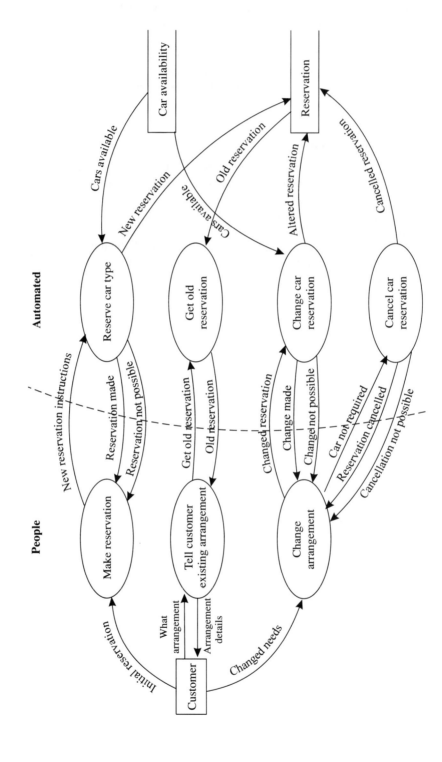

Figure 4.4 Reservations data flow diagram: functional primitive level.

handles a customer's initial approach and subsequent changes of mind. The *automated* part specifies the machine processes of storing and retrieving the information.

In this example the flows that cross between the *people* part and the *automated* part are:

1. New reservation instructions
2. Reservation made
3. Reservation not possible
4. Get old reservation
5. Old reservation
6. Changed reservation
7. Change made
8. Change not possible
9. Car not required
10. Reservation cancelled
11. Cancellation not possible

On examination it can be deduced that flows 2 and 3 are a response to 1 (the fact a reservation has been made or is not possible depends on an attempt to make such a reservation) and thus these can be grouped and identified as a logical transaction. Similarly:

4 and 5
6, 7 and 8
9, 10 and 11

also all form logical transactions. Thus, in this part of the system there are four logical transactions:

1. Make a reservation
2. Obtain reservation details for a change
3. Change a reservation
4. Delete a reservation

Each one of these could be performed in isolation from the others and is therefore discrete. They all either change or retrieve held data. After completion of any one of them system integrity will have been maintained and the business supported.

4.3.4 Function decomposition

At the bottom level of a function decomposition hierarchy are the fundamental processes that define what is to be done in the system. Not all the bottom level functions will be logical transactions, but they can be used to help identify logical transactions.

Clearly, from Fig. 4.5 it is almost impossible to ascertain the logical transactions that are represented. However, when taken in conjunction with the DFDs the 'right leg' of view 1 (i.e. the components of *Record customer requirements*) seem to represent logical transactions. In view 2, however, there does not appear to be a simple correlation.

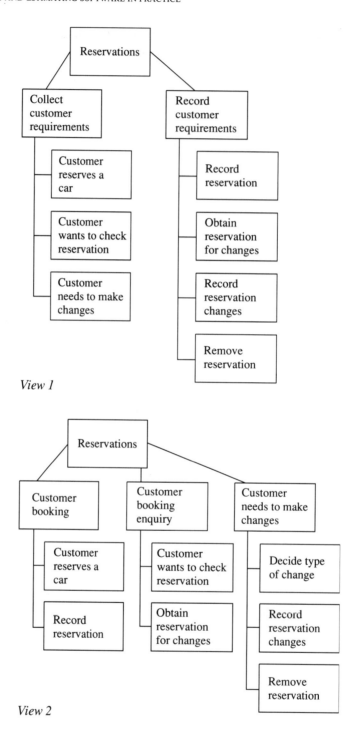

Figure 4.5 Two views of the functional decomposition of 'Reservations'.

The problem with functional decomposition diagrams, from a function point analysis point of view, is that they do not show either information flow or access paths. Given this, it is suggested that these hierarchies, on their own, are not enough to be able to measure the system.

4.3.5 The data approach

The process of data analysis is essentially one of producing systems models of the relevant portion of the business from a data point of view, firstly by modelling the information to be held, and secondly by examining how events in business affect that information. It is the second step of this process that results in the production of a document that is extremely useful to the function point counter, the event/entity cross-reference matrix, sometimes known as the 'CRUD' (Create, Reference, Update, Delete) matrix. This matrix shows how events in the real world, which affect the business, also have an effect on stored data. An example is given in Fig. 4.6.

	Car type	Tariff	Reservation	Customer	Account Customer	Customer Agreement	User	User type	User privileges
Make reservation	R	R	C	C	R	R			
Reservation enquiry	R		R	R					
Change reservation	R	R	U	U	R	R			
Cancel reservation	R		D	R			R	R	R

Figure 4.6 Event/entity cross-reference for 'Reservations'.

Examination of this matrix immediately shows how the *events* correspond to logical transactions. These events are caused by combinations of circumstances which mean that the user will need to communicate with the system. If these matrices have been reduced to the correct level they are an exact indication of logical transactions.

4.3.6 Identifying input and output components

The input and output components of a transaction are the parts that receive data into the system and pass it back out again. What we are interested in is information that passes across the system boundary, that is across the division between what will be automated and what will not.

The easiest and most obvious place to identify this is in the data flow diagrams. Referring back to Fig. 4.4, the transactions and their input and output components can therefore be identified as:

1. Make a'reservation
   Has an input flow:

   > *New reservation instructions*

   and output flows:

   > *Reservation made*
   > *Reservation not possible*

2. Obtain reservation details for a change
   Has an input flow:

   > *Get old reservation*

   and an output flow:

   > *Old reservation*

3. Change a reservation
   Has an input flow:

   > *Changed reservation*

   and output flows:

   > *Change made*
   > *Change not possible*

4. Delete a reservation.
   Has an input flow:

   > *Car not required*

   and output flows:

   > *Reservation cancelled*
   > *Cancellation not possible*

4.3.7 What do you do if there are no data flow diagrams?

The answer to this question is dependent on the documentation that you actually have available:

- Is there documentation that defines input and output in another way, i.e. is there documentation that describes the system's expected response to events?
- Is there documentation that describes the entities that are being processed by the transactions?

Documentation which identifies input and output in the absence of DFDs

There may be alternatives to data flow diagrams, used in some methodologies, which are provided for the same purpose but which are called by some other name. Any diagram that shows the system boundary and data entering and leaving the system can be used for identifying the input and output data. Remember that it is the input and output to logical transactions that we are interested in, i.e. data that is grouped into sets that can be identified by the user as complete and discrete.

Table 4.1 shows a 'conversation' table of a type that may be used in place of data flow diagrams. From this the transactions can be identified from the event descriptions, the inputs from the user actions and the outputs from the system responses.

Table 4.1 User and system actions in response to an event

Event	User action	System response
1. Customer reserves car	(a) Reservation details	(a) Creates reservation
		(b) Passes back result
2. Wants to know about reservation	(a) Reservation identification	(a) Passes back reservation details
3. Wants to revise reservation	(a) New reservation details	(a) Changes reservation
		(b) Passes back result
4. Does not require car	(a) Reservation identification	(a) Deletes reservation
		(b) Passes back result

Documentation which describes the entities that are handled by transactions

If a purely data analysis approach has been adopted it is possible that only an event/ entity cross-reference matrix has been produced. In this case the identification of inputs and outputs is not difficult, but the sizing of them might be.

By definition, all logical transactions have input and output components: the fact that a transaction has been identified means that the components of that transaction can be identified. A starting point to sizing in these circumstances is to consider the attributes of the entities processed by the transaction. The difficulty comes with accounting for derived fields, such as totals, which may not be obvious from the documentation since they may only be implied in the event description.

What if none of the above is available?

We have addressed this question to some extent already. If there really is no documentation available during development that allows you to identify inputs and outputs, then the question has to be asked: 'How will you know that the system is fit for purpose?'.

4.3.8 Identifying entities accessed

By this stage of development an entity model should have been produced to show the entities that are needed to support the system. If the model has been normalized, the entities will have been reduced to *third normal form*, that is split into logically separate units of data. We can see an example of such a model in Fig. 4.7, which shows the model in a slightly different state from the one drawn at the start of the project. Notice that an entity *account customer* has now been identified. It is, in fact,

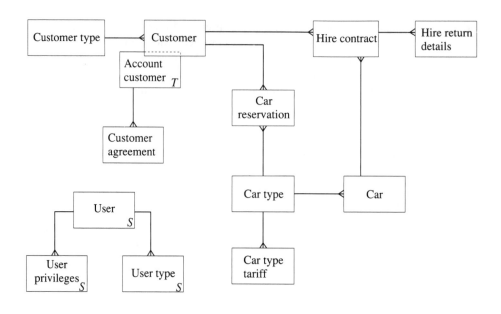

Account customer:	Account identifier
Car:	Registration, Make, Model, Type
Car type:	Type, No. passengers, No. doors, Description
Car type tariff:	Type, Start date, End date, Weekly charge, Daily charge, Mileage charge
Car reservation:	Customer, Car type, Start date, End date, Agreed weekly rate, Agreed daily rate, Agreed mileage charge, Agreed maximum, Comments
Customer:	Customer name, Company name, Customer type, Customer address, Customer postcode, Billing address, Driving licence number, Date of birth, Comments
Customer agreement:	Account number, Salesperson, Date of agreement, Negotiated weekly charge, Negotiated daily charge, Negotiated mileage charge, Start date, End date, Comments
Customer type:	Type, Description
Hire contract:	Customer, Car, Booking car type, Booking start date, Actual start date, End date, Contracted weekly rate, Contracted daily rate, Contracted mileage charge, Contracted maximum, Comments
Hire return details:	Customer, Car, Actual start date, Actual end date, No. weeks charged for, No. days charged for, No. miles charged for, Comments
User:	User password, User name, User type
User privileges:	User type, Facility, Access level
User type:	User type, Description

Figure 4.7 Car hire front desk entity model.

a subtype of *customer*. Notice also three entities *user*, *user type* and *user privileges*: these control the system security and as such are counted as part of the system entity.

Before counting the entities accessed by each transaction it is necessary to categorize the entities on the entity model. In Fig. 4.7 the category to which an entity belongs has been indicated by a letter in the bottom right-hand corner of the box:

    T   Subtype
    S   System entity
    blank Primary entity

How are entities identified from the event/entity cross-reference matrix?

This is simplicity itself: for each event, list those entities that are subject to a *create*, *read*, *update* or *delete*. Note that we are only interested in the entities, not the way that they are accessed. Some methodologies may show that an entity is referenced and updated, whereas we would only list the entity once.

If an entity is subject to two different amendment type accesses (e.g. it is created and updated by a single event), then the model has not been decomposed to the correct level. A single event will not cause the user to want to create and amend the same information.

What if there is no event/entity cross-reference matrix?

All is not lost: there is just more work to do. Other supporting documentation could be used:

Data store/entity cross-reference matrix
Data dictionary data flow descriptions
Entity descriptions

Data store/entity cross-reference matrix   If a transaction accesses a data store, then find the entities that are associated with that store and list them. It may appear that this is the simplest route to take, but there are problems:

1. The transaction may not access all the entities held on the data store. Just because there is a flow from a data store it does not follow that all the entities referenced by that data store contribute to the flow.
2. The relationship between data stores and entities may be many to many, i.e. a data store may contain many entities and an entity may appear in many data stores.

These problems mean that a conclusive list for a logical transaction cannot be drawn up solely from this piece of documentation. While the list produced by this method is a subset of the whole model, it will contain all the entities that *could* be accessed by the transaction as opposed to those that actually are.

Data dictionary, data flow descriptions and entity descriptions   A more accurate, if more time-consuming method, is to examine the contents of the data flows into and out of the transaction. These data flows contain field descriptions that should map directly onto entity attributes (or derivatives of them, e.g. totals). If they do not, the models are inconsistent and further examination of the system is necessary.

On looking at the example data dictionary entry in Fig. 4.8, and examining the first data flow *New reservation instructions*, it can be seen that the entities

Car type
Reservation
Customer
Account customer

hold the attributes onto which the input fields map.

Data dictionary for: Car hire front desk
Data flow description: New reservation instructions
From: Make a reservation **To:** Reserve car type
Contents: Customer name, Car type, Start date, End date, Customer account number, Agreed maximum, Comments

Data dictionary for: Car hire front desk
Data flow description: Reservation made
From: Reserve car type **To:** Make a reservation
Contents: Customer name, Car type, Start date, End date, Agreed weekly rate, Agreed daily rate, Agreed mileage charge, Agreed maximum, Comments

Data dictionary for: Car hire front desk
Data flow description: Reservation not possible
From: Reserve car type **To:** Make a reservation
Contents: Customer name, Car type, Start date, End date, Reason for failure

---

Figure 4.8 Data flow descriptions for the transaction 'Make a reservation'.

The second data flow, *Reservation made*, contains the additional fields *Agreed weekly rate*, *Agreed daily rate* and *Agreed mileage charge*. These are stored on the *reservation* entity created by this transaction. Since they were not input by the user they must have been read from other entities in the system. Two entities store such information, and therefore the information must have been read from at least one of them: these are *tariff* and *customer agreement*. Further investigation would establish that if the customer has a *customer agreement* the rates are obtained from there, otherwise the standard *tariff* rates are used; thus both must be listed.

The final data flow *reservation not possible* is an error message and requires access to no other entities than those already identified.

The final entity list for this example is therefore:

Car type
Reservation
Customer
Account customer
Customer agreement
Tariff

4.4 SIZING THE TRANSACTIONS

The following is a brief review of the rules for sizing. For fuller details refer to Chapter 2.

4.4.1 Input and output

To establish the size of input and output count the fields identified in the previous step. If a field is shown on more than one component count it for each time it appears. For example, in Fig. 4.8 *customer name* appears on all three flows: it is counted once for input and twice for output. If there is a reason for the field to be output after input, e.g. the user wants it printed or highlighted, then it contributes to both input and output. If there is no reason then the documentation should not show that it is output and input.

4.4.2 Entities

It is not enough simply to count the entities: the three different types of entity are handled differently.

- Primary entities: count them all (they all contribute to the processing when accessed).
- Subtypes: these are only counted if they are handled differently from the other subtypes of their parent primary entity. For instance, in *make reservation* and *change reservation* the rates for account customers are obtained differently from those for ordinary customers. The entity *account customer* is therefore included in the count.
- System entity: this entity does not strictly exist in a logical model but some methodologies may show it. It contains information that is necessary for the computer system to operate: e.g. in our case study *user*, *user type* and *user privileges* are only required by the computer system. They are there to prevent inappropriate operation of the computer system. No matter how many of these system entities are accessed by a transaction, only one is added to its count.

4.5 UNADJUSTED FUNCTION POINTS

If the transactions and their components identified on the worksheet shown in Fig. 4.1 are sized using the above rules and the additional information in Figs 4.8 and 4.9, a transaction counting worksheet can be completed, as shown in Fig. 4.10.

Data dictionary for: Car hire front desk
Data flow description: Get old reservation
From: Tell customer existing arrangement **To:** Get old reservation
Contents: Customer name, Car type, Start Date

Data dictionary for: Car hire front desk
Data flow description: Old reservation
From: Get old reservation **To:** Tell customer existing arrangement
Contents: Customer, Customer name, Car type, Car type description, Start Date, End date, Agreed weekly rate, Agreed daily rate, Agreed mileage charge, Agree maximum, Comments

Data dictionary for: Car hire front desk
Data flow description: Changed reservation
From: Change arrangements **To:** Change car reservation
Contents: Customer, Customer name, Car type, Start Date, End date, Agreed weekly rate, Agreed daily rate, Agreed mileage charge, Agree maximum, Comments

---

Figure 4.9 continued over

Figure 4.9 continued

Data dictionary for: Car hire front desk
Data flow description: Change made
From: Change car reservations **To:** Change arrangement
Contents: Customer, Customer name, Car type, Car type description, Start Date, End date, Agreed weekly rate, Agreed daily rate, Agreed mileage charge, Agree maximum, Comments

Data dictionary for: Car hire front desk
Data flow description: Change not possible
From: Change car reservations **To:** Change arrangement
Contents: Customer, Customer name, Car type, Car type description, Start Date, End date, Agreed weekly rate, Agreed daily rate, Agreed mileage charge, Agree maximum, Comments, Error message

Data dictionary for: Car hire front desk
Data flow description: Car not required
From: Change arrangement **To:** Cancel car reservation
Contents: Customer name, Car type, Start Date

Data dictionary for: Car hire front desk
Data flow description: Reservation cancelled
From: Cancel car reservation **To:** Change arrangements
Contents: Customer, Customer name, Car type, Car type description, Start Date, End date, Reservation cancelled message

Data dictionary for: Car hire front desk
Data flow description: Cancellation not possible
From: Cancel car reservation **To:** Change arrangement
Contents: Customer name, Car type, Start Date, Error message

Figure 4.9 Data flow contents.

Transaction indentification worksheet

SYSTEM: *Car hire*
SYSTEM AREA: *Reservations*
SOURCE DOCUMENTATION: DFD, CRUD, *Data dictionary*

Transaction	Input	Entities	Output
1. *Make a reservation*	7	6	14
2. *Obtain reservation details for a change*	3	3	11
3. *Change a reservation*	10	6	23
4. *Delete a reservation*	3	4	11
Total	23	19	59

Figure 4.10 Transaction counting worksheet

To calculate the unadjusted function points apply an appropriate set of weights, in this case the industry standard:

$$
\begin{array}{lll}
\text{Input} & 23 \times 0.58 = & 13.34 \\
\text{Entities} & 19 \times 1.66 = & 31.54 \\
\text{Output} & 59 \times 0.26 = & 15.34 \\
& \textit{Total} & 60.22
\end{array}
$$

4.6 SCORING TECHNICAL COMPLEXITY FACTORS

The next step in sizing the system involves the assessment of technical complexity (detailed rules are listed in Appendix A: see also Chapter 2).

It was pointed out earlier that, in addition to information requirements (or functional requirements in SSADM), the logical design will contain some criteria (in SSADM, non-functional requirements) that will enable the designers to produce a system that works quickly enough, is robust enough etc. These are sometimes known as the quality aspects of the system (although strictly speaking quality has a wider definition). They are system requirements not concerned with information content, not arising from the project environment, but nonetheless affecting the size of the task.

Examination of these criteria enables the technical complexity to be scored. Figure 4.11 gives an example statement of the non-functional requirements for the car hire front desk system.

Other user requirements

Performance
The reception clerks need the system to respond quickly: they are dealing with the general public who want to know that the company are capable of supplying a service in a reliable manner. All customer interactions must be immediate and accurate.

Sales and Accounts operate in a similar way: when they have made an agreement with a customer then it must take effect straightaway.

Accounts require periodic reports of payments.

Management need to be able to change tariffs quickly. Their reports are required periodically.

Volumes
It is expected that the system will have to handle 100 hirings a week (enquiries result in a 20% takeup).

Reliability and maintenance
The system is to be 'turnkey': there will be no technical staff on site. The suppliers of the system will have a remote diagnostic and maintenance facility.

The system should be operable throughout the working day. Should there be a failure – twice a year maximum – then the system should be operable again within 1 hour.

Ease of use and training
The system should be self-explanatory. Staff should be able to teach themselves the system from a tutorial and the user documentation. It should not be possible for the staff to get stuck: help should be available to enable them to do what they want to do.

Figure 4.11 Car hire front desk system: non-functional requirements.

4.7 WORKED EXAMPLE: SCORING THE TECHNICAL COMPLEXITY OF THE CAR HIRE SYSTEM

1. *Data communications*
   It is suggested by the requirements that the system will need to be implemented with terminals for front desk, accounts and sales. Though there will be an element of batch processing (e.g. report production) the majority of the system will be on-line. Most systems written in recent years, other than single user PC applications, will score 4 or 5 for this category.
   This system scores:

   4   More than front-end, but only 1 TP comms protocol

2. *Distributed data processing*
   There is no indication that distributed processing will feature in this system; therefore the score is:

   0   Application does not aid transfer of data or processing between components of system

3. *Performance*
   There are performance considerations for this system, but nothing out of the ordinary. The scoring criteria for this category suggest a score of 2 or 3. However, it is more than 2 because the processing deadline is immediate, not the next business day, and it is less than 3, because there are no interfacing systems. In this case opt for:

   3   On-line response critical during business day. No special design for CPU utilization. Processing deadline affected by interfacing systems.

4. *Heavily used configuration*
   This is a 'turnkey' system; therefore the score is:

   0   Dedicated target configuration

5. *Transaction rates*
   Though the number of transactions is mentioned, there is no indication of peaks; score:

   0   No peak anticipated

6. *On-line data entry*
   From the user requirements, on-line data entry is essential for practically all input. Most recent systems will be similar. Score:

   5   >30% interactive

7. *End-user efficiency*
   The ease of use requirement shows that the system needs to be self-sufficient, i.e. users require on-line functions to help in the use of the system. Of the types of facility listed this system would require at least six. Score:

   3   >6 of the above

8. *On-line update*
The requirements suggest that the system will need to reflect the real world but, as systems software will suffice, score as:

1   On-line update is provided by systems software

9. *Complex processing*
There is no complex processing suggested by this system; score:

0   None

10. *Usable in other applications*
At first it appears there is no specific reference to the reusability of the code. However, the system is being written as a *turnkey* package, so any supplier producing such a system will have an eye on other customers; score:

4   Application was specifically packaged/documented to aid reuse, and application customized at source code level

11. *Installation ease*
Not mentioned, but there must be existing information to be taken on; score:

1   No special conversion and installation considerations were stated by the user, but special setup required for installation

12. *Operations ease*
As a turnkey system score:

5   Application is designed for unattended operation. This means no operator intervention other than start-up and shutdown. Error recovery is automatic

13. *Multiple sites*
There is no mention of many sites; score:

0   No user requirement to consider the needs of more than one user site

14. *Facilitate change*
Though maintenance was mentioned, there is no indication that the requirements are volatile or that changes may be needed. Anyway, this category is geared towards scoring for flexible report generating and enquiry facilities. Score:

0   No special user requirement to design the application to minimize or facilitate change

15. *Requirements of other applications*
There are no interfacing applications. Score:

0   The system is completely standalone

16. *Security, privacy, auditability*
Though not mentioned, it is probable that the user categories will not have access to each other's functions; also an accounting system will require audit. Score:

> 1   for meeting personal (maybe legal) privacy requirements
> 1   for meeting special auditability requirements
> = 2   Total

17. *User training needs*
    Users will require training (in fact they will need to teach themselves); score:

    4   On-line training course material provided

18. *Direct use by third parties*
    Third parties, in this sense, means people other than those within the organization and identified as users during analysis, e.g. bank customers using an ATM. This system will only be operated by the company's staff; score:

    0   No third party connection to the system

19. *Documentation*
    The development method for this system is unknown. However, from the fact that FPA is being carried out, and from documents seen so far, it can be deduced that the following are probably available:

    > User requirements definition
    > User design (logical design/functional design)
    > Technical design
    > Program documentation (at least flow charts)
    > Data element library
    > Data element/record/program cross-reference
    > Operations manual
    > User manual
    > Test data library
    > Change request/error report log

    Count 1 for each document type listed = 10. Score:

    4   If 9–10 documentation types

Having scored each of the 19 factors, it is necessary to sum them to give the total degrees of influence (D_{oI}):

$$\text{Total degrees of influence} = 36$$

and then to calculate the technical complexity adjustment (TCA) factor as

$$
\begin{aligned}
\text{TCA} &= 0.65 + (D_{oI} \times 0.005) \\
&= 0.65 + (36 \times 0.005) \\
&= 0.83
\end{aligned}
$$

4.8 TECHNICAL COMPLEXITY – A WORD OF WARNING

Unadjusted function points are calculated by a rigorous process of counting, which means that, given a set of documentation that is correct (a complete logical model of the system, decomposed to the correct level), there is no room for interpretation: one counter will get the same result as another.

Technical complexity adjustment, as can be seen from the above, involves a degree of judgement. This can and will result in different people getting different results. Where there is concern about possible variations of interpretation while assessing technical complexity and it is felt that the variation would be severe enough to cause a significant variation in the function point index (normally an unlikely situation), assessment should be carried out by an informed group and the result agreed.

4.9 THE FINAL CALCULATION

To produce the function point index the information processing dimension must be combined with that representing technical complexity:

Function point index = Unadjusted function points × TCA

In our example, only part of the car hire system has been counted, but a function point index can be produced for that section:

FPI for reservations = 60.22 × 0.83 = 49.98

Note: Given the possible variations in TCA due to interpretation, as well as the fact that FPA is really only a good first-order measure (i.e. gives an answer that is reasonably accurate but not totally precise), the size should be rounded, in this example to 50 function points. Arguably, rounding to the nearest 5 for small counts (say < 100 fpts) or 10 for larger systems would give a number that can be quoted more meaningfully with less room for spurious precision where none really exists. Obviously, if the size is being used in calculations (e.g. estimating or performance measurement) then there is no point in introducing unnecessary errors by rounding the size prior to use in such calculations.

Because MKII function points are additive in nature, the project can be analysed section by section and the results accumulated to produce an overall system size.

4.10 POTENTIAL PROBLEMS AND THEIR SOLUTIONS

4.10.1 I'm still unclear about 'A model of the logical system'

A model of the logical system is simply a representation of the user requirements. Different methodologies may specify different approaches to logical modelling. The logical model may be a textual list of functionality required, or it could be built up from logical data models and logical data flow diagrams.

4.10.2 What is meant by 'sufficient decomposition'?

As we said earlier, for our purposes the model should be decomposed to at least logical transaction level. If there are logical transactions containing highly complex algorithms, it may be worth decomposing further. What is important is that the reader is aware that models may not be at the correct level for logical transactions to be read off the model directly. It is difficult to say when a system has been decomposed too far, and it is not within the scope of this book to set rules: there are many excellent publications describing systems analysis techniques.

A model that is at too high a level to make logical transactions easy to identify can quickly be spotted, and Figs 4.12 and 4.13 are example representations of 'Reservations' that have not been reduced to the appropriate level. In these examples the part of the system that has been examined throughout this chapter is shown at too high a level for accurate function point measurement. There are two major giveaways:

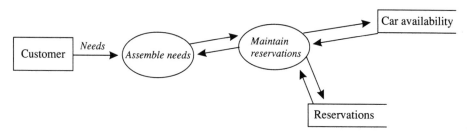

Figure 4.12 DFD for Reservations.

	Car type	Tariff	Reservation	Customer	Account customer	Customer agreement	User	User type	User privileges
Maintain reservation	R	R	CRUD	CRU	R	R	R	R	R

Figure 4.13 Event/entity matrix of Reservations.

1. The word 'maintain': this usually means 'add', 'amend', 'delete' and 'enquire'.
2. Events that create, update and delete are usually composite: that is they consist of several discrete events.

When encountering documentation at too high a level, further analysis is required. This strictly speaking is not the job of function point analysts, although all too often they are forced to do it.

4.10.3 What happens when the data models and function models do not match?

This probably means that someone has not done their job properly. They both describe the same system therefore they *should* match.

If one model shows a different number or type of logical transactions then more work is needed to make them consistent. Again, this is not the job of the function-point analyst.

4.11 CONCLUSION

This chapter has examined how to count function points given a logical system design, the proper vehicle for measurement. In addition to providing a useful size metric, this exercise provides valuable integrity checking: if the models/documents do not allow accurate identification and sizing of the logical transactions then they do not constitute a logical design. Effectively, 'if you've got it, you can measure it; if you haven't, you can't'.

Sizing the system using models produced before or after the logical design involves a degree of estimation. To find out about estimation techniques see Chapter 3 or Chapter 5.

4.12 KEY POINTS

- The system is typically resized during the project in order to provide control information for managers, project leaders etc.
- The resizing is carried out using the logical model, i.e. the document which details what will be implemented, not how it will be done.
- Systems can be sized from a number of models. If the models are adequate and correctly describe the same system then the resultant sizes will be the same, whichever model is used

4.13 CASE STUDY: GENERAL PRACTITIONER'S PATIENT CONTACT SYSTEM

For general notes on case studies please see the introductory text to the case study in Chapter 3.

4.13.1 Task

Measure the size of the administration facilities in the system using:

- Data flow diagrams (Figs 4.14–4.18)
- Entity model (Fig. 4.19, Table 4.2)
- Data dictionary details (Table 4.3)
- Data store/entity cross-reference
- CRUD matrix (Fig. 4.20)

Sample solutions are to be found in Appendix C.

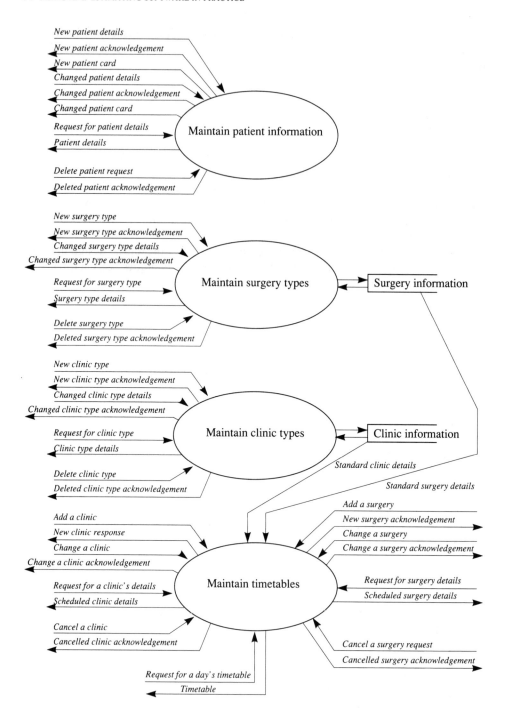

Figure 4.14 The patient contact system: administration functions, high-level DFD.

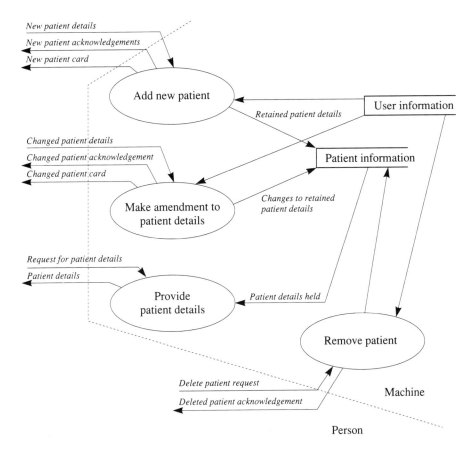

Figure 4.15 Maintain patient details: detailed DFD.

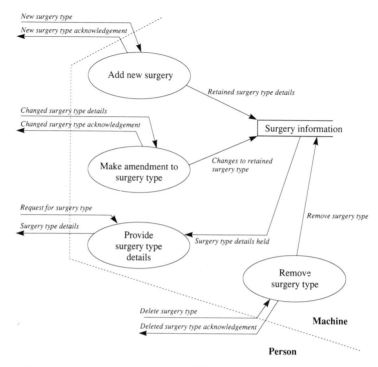

Figure 4.16 Maintain surgery type: detailed DFD.

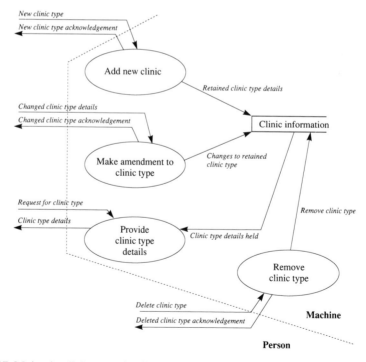

Figure 4.17 Maintain clinic type: detailed DFD.

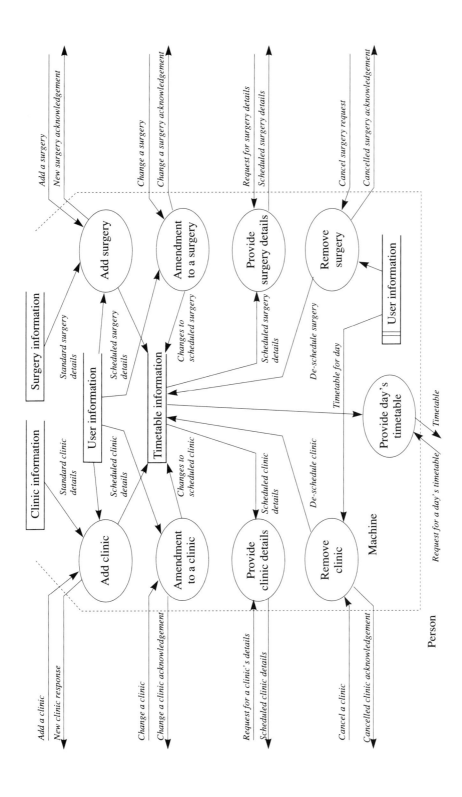

Figure 4.18 Maintain timetable: detailed DFD.

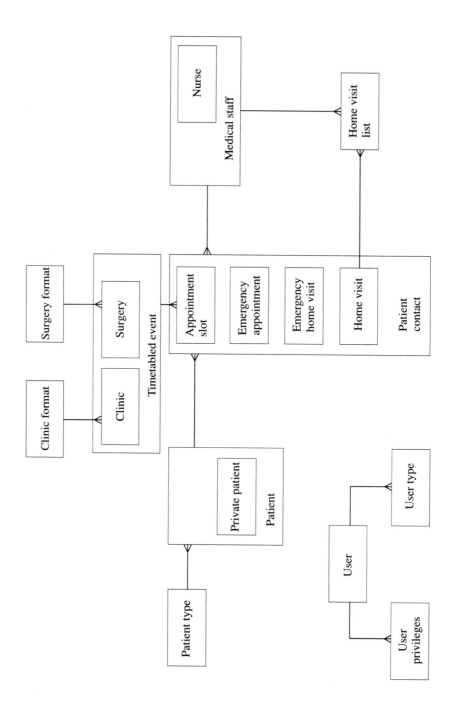

Figure 4.19 Patient contacts: entity model.

Table 4.2 Entity descriptions

Entity	Description	Attributes
Appointment slot	Booked appointment at a surgery or clinic	Time of slot, timetabled event
Clinic	A scheduled clinic	Type of clinic, type of patient invited, invitation letter text
Clinic format	Standard format for clinic	Clinic type, Clinic name, Normal clinic duration, Slot length, Type of medic responsible, Type of patient expected, Standard invitation letter text
Emergency appointment	Appointment outside normal surgery run	Reason for emergency appointment
Emergency home visit	An non-appointment visit by a doctor to a patient at home	Expected duration, Actual duration, Address for visit, Reason for emergency visit
Home visit	A booked visit by a medical staff member to a patient at home	Expected duration, Actual duration, Address for visit
Home visit list	Booked visits a medical staff member is to make on a particular day	Date, Scheduled medic
Medical staff	A member of the practice who can treat patients	Name, Type of staff, Address, Telephone number, Comments
Nurse	A type of medical staff with nursing qualifications	Midwife indicator
Patient	A person treated by the practice	Patient identifier (NHS, NI number or other), Patient name, Patient type code, Patient type description, NHS number, NI number, DOB, Address, Telephone number
Patient contact	A contact between a patient and a member of the medical staff	Date, Time, Patient identifier, Medic identifier, Type of contact
Private patient	A patient who is dealt with on a private basis; may or may not have an NHS or NI number	Billing method, NHS, NI or other Indicator
Patient type	Describes type of patient	Patient type code, Description
Surgery	A scheduled surgery	Surgery type
Surgery format	Standard format for surgery	Surgery type, Normal duration, Slot length, Type of medic responsible
Timetabled event	Scheduled group of patient contacts	Date, Type of event, Start time, End time, Length of slots, Medic responsible
User	A person who has access to the computer system	User name, Title, User type code, Position
User privileges	Access rights for a particular user	Logon code, Privilege level
User type	Describes a user type	User type code

Table 4.3 Data dictionary

External flow	Description	Fields
Add a clinic	Details of a new clinic being added to a daily timetable	Date of timetable, Type of clinic, Start time, End time, Medic responsible
Add a surgery	Details of a new surgery being added to a daily timetable	Date of timetable, Standard surgery type, Start time, End time, Doctor responsible
Cancel a surgery	Remove a clinic from a daily timetable	Date of timetable, Start time
Cancelled surgery acknowledgement	Message giving result of surgery cancellation	Date of timetable, Time of surgery, Response message (success or failure)
Change a clinic	Details of a change to a scheduled clinic	Date of timetable, Type of clinic, Start time, End time, Medic responsible, Length of slots
Change a clinic acknowledgement	Acknowledgement message giving result of change to a scheduled clinic	Date of timetable, Start time, End time, Medic responsible, Length of slots, Response message (success or failure)
Change a surgery	Details of a change to scheduled surgery	Date of timetable, Type of surgery, Start time, End time, Medic responsible, Length of slots
Change a surgery acknowledgement	Message giving result of change to a scheduled surgery	Date of timetable, Start time, End time, Doctor responsible, Length of slots, Response message (success or failure)
Changed clinic type acknowledgement	Message giving result of change to a standard clinic	Clinic type, Clinic name, Normal clinic duration, Slot length, Invitation letter text, Response message (success or failure)
Changed clinic type details	Details of changes to be made to a standard clinic	Clinic type, Clinic name, Type of medic responsible, Type of patient, Normal clinic duration, Slot length, Invitation letter text
Changed patient acknowledgement	Message giving result of change to a patient's details	Patient name, NHS number, NI number, DOB, Address, Telephone number, Response message (success or failure)
Changed patient card	Hard copy of changed patient details	Patient name, NHS number, NI number, DOB, Address, Telephone number
Changed patient details	Changed patient details	Patient name, NHS number, NI number, DOB, Address, Telephone number
Changed surgery type acknowledgement	Message giving result of change to a standard surgery	Surgery type, Normal duration, Slot length, Type of medic responsible, Response message (success or failure)
Changed surgery type details	Details of changes to be made to a standard surgery	Surgery type, Normal duration, Slot length, Type of medic responsible
Clinic type details	Details of a standard clinic	Clinic type, Clinic name, Type of medic responsible, Type of patient, Normal duration, Slot length, Invitation letter text
Timetable	Timetable for a particular day	Date, Clinic type, Clinic start time, Clinic end time, Medic responsible for clinic, Surgery type, Surgery start time, Surgery end time, Medic responsible for surgery

External flow	Description	Fields
Cancel clinic	Remove a clinic from a daily timetable	Date of timetable, Type of clinic, Start time
Cancel clinic acknowledgement	Message giving result of clinic cancellation	Date of timetable, Type of clinic, Response message (success or failure)
Deleted clinic type acknowledgement	Message giving result of removal of a standard clinic	Clinic type, Clinic description, Response message (success or failure)
Deleted patient acknowledgement	Message giving result of removal of a standard clinic	Patient name, Patient NHS number, Patient address, Response message (success or failure)
Deleted surgery type acknowledgement	Message giving result of removal of a standard surgery	Surgery type, Surgery description, Response message (success or failure)
Delete clinic type request	Details of standard clinic for removal	Clinic type
Delete patient request	Details of patient for removal	Patient NHS number
Delete surgery type	Details of standard surgery for removal	Surgery type
New clinic response	Message giving result of adding a scheduled clinic	Date of timetable, Type of clinic, Medic responsible, Start time, End time, Length of slots, Response message (success or failure)
New clinic type acknowledgement	Message giving result of addition of a standard clinic	Clinic type, Clinic name, Normal clinic duration, Slot length, Invitation letter text, response message (success or failure)
New clinic type	Details of a new standard clinic	Clinic type, Clinic name, Normal clinic duration, Slot length, Invitation letter text
New patient acknowledgement	Message giving result of adding a new patient	Patient name, NHS number, NI number, DOB, Address, Telephone number, response message (success or failure)
New patient card	Hard copy of new patient details	Patient name, NHS number, NI number, DOB, Address, Telephone number
New patient details	Details of a patient new to the practice	Patient name, Patient type, NHS number, NI number, DOB, Address, Telephone number
New surgery acknowledgement	Message giving result of adding a scheduled surgery	Date of timetable, Type of surgery, Medic responsible, Start time, End time, Length of slots, Response message (success or failure)
New surgery type acknowledgement	Message giving result of addition of a standard surgery	Surgery type, Normal surgery duration, Slot length, Type of medic responsible, Response message (success or failure)
New surgery type	Details of a new standard surgery	Surgery type, Normal surgery duration, Slot length, Type of medic responsible, Response message (success or failure)
Patient details	Details of a patient	Patient name, Patient type, Patient type description, NHS number, NI number, DOB, Address, Telephone number
Request for a clinic's details	Request to retrieve and display the details of a scheduled clinic	Date, Clinic type, Clinic start time

External flow	Description	Fields
Request for a day's timetable	Request to output a timetable for a particular day	Date
Request for surgery details	Request to retrieve and display the details of a scheduled surgery	Date, Surgery type, Start time
Request for clinic type	Request to retrieve and display the details of a standard clinic	Clinic type
Request for patient details	Request for the output of a patient's details	Patient NHS number
Request for surgery type	Request to retrieve and display the details of a standard surgery	Surgery type
Scheduled clinic details	Details of a scheduled clinic	Date of timetable, Type of clinic, Start time, End time, Medic responsible, Length of slots, Invitation letter text
Scheduled surgery details	Details of a scheduled surgery	Date of timetable, Type of surgery, Start time, End time, Medic responsible, Length of slots
Surgery type details	Details of a new standard surgery	Surgery type, Normal surgery duration, Slot length, Type of medic responsible

	Clinic	Clinic format	Patient	Patient type	Surgery	Surgery format	Timetabled event	Appointment slot	User	User type	User privileges
New patient			C	R					R		R
Change to patient			U	R					R		R
Patient enquiry			R	R							
Patient leaves			D					R	R		R
New surgery type						C					
Change to surgery type						U					
Surgery type enquiry						R					
Surgery type redundant					R	D					
New clinic type		C									
Change to clinic type		U									
Clinic type enquiry		R									
Clinic type redundant	R	D									
Schedule a clinic	C	R					C				
Schedule a surgery					C	R	C				
Scheduled clinic changed	U	R					U				
Scheduled surgery changed					U	R	U				
Scheduled clinic enquiry		R					R				
Scheduled surgery enquiry					R		R				
Clinic cancelled	D						D	R			
Surgery cancelled					D		D	R			
Produce day's timetable							R				

Figure 4.20 CRUD matrix for patient contact system.

5

SIZING DELIVERED AND EXISTING SYSTEMS

5.1 INTRODUCTION

The purpose of this chapter is to explain how to size implemented systems, i.e. both those systems that have been recently completed as well as those systems developed at some point in the past. The need to size these systems is examined briefly and then suggestions made as to how best to approach the task and also how to deal with some of the common difficulties encountered.

By the end of the chapter the reader should have a basic understanding of the need for sizing these systems, have an understanding of a basic approach to their sizing, know of some of the more common difficulties that can arise, and be able to size the majority of implemented systems that they encounter (with reference to external help for more complex systems).

5.1.1 Why size systems already completed?

Implemented systems need to be sized for a variety of reasons, typically:

- To establish the size of the IT portfolio for assessing and monitoring IS support performance
- To establish a database of measures of the IS development process performance, usually with a view to improving future performance
- To monitor, measure and improve the effectiveness of the IS estimating process

The uses of the size measure are explored in more detail in Chapter 7.

5.1.2 What are the difficulties with sizing existing systems?

The sizing of existing systems is prone to error. The major problem areas are:

- The original requirements and design documents may not have been kept up to date, if they have been kept at all.
- Logical models will have been altered in order to optimize them for physical design considerations.
- Confusion can arise over the difference between physical computer transactions and logical transactions.
- Input and output fields may contain control information, such as screen navigation and menus, as opposed to business data.

All this can make life very difficult for the function-point analyst. There is, however, a basic approach that can be followed, and some techniques that can be applied in order to minimize the difficulties.

5.1.3 A basic approach to sizing

What is offered in this section is a tried and trusted approach that works very well for the people who use it. The actual approach that you take is very much a matter for your personal choice, and will evolve as you gain experience with the method.

Stage 1: decide who should be involved

The first stage is to identify who is to be involved in the sizing exercise. Ideally the person who is doing the function point count should be an experienced function-point analyst with strong analysis skills, and also be someone who is familiar with the details of the functionality of the system to be sized. This ideal situation rarely occurs of course, and the next best option is for the experienced function-point analyst, as described above, to work with someone who has the required knowledge of the system to be sized. Anything less than this will usually either make the sizing process prohibitively expensive or result in erroneous sizing.

Stage 2: three steps in sizing a system

In this basic approach there are three steps to sizing. The description accompanying each step assumes an experienced function-point analyst is working with someone who is knowledgeable about the system, and the description has been written from the point of view of the function-point analyst. The steps are of course applicable where only one person is involved, and the thought processes implied by the descriptions will be similar.

1. *Identify logical transactions*
   The first step is to create a list of logical transactions. The easiest way to do this is to work in a top-down fashion, starting with the person who knows the system providing an overview description of its functionality, and then repeatedly breaking this down until the functionality is being described at a logical transaction level.
   Listening is the key here: spot words like *maintain* which usually hide *updates*, *adds* and *deletes*, and watch out for *enquire before* type transactions as well. Each of these is a separate transaction. (Enquire before transactions are explained

later in this chapter in the *Menu screens* section.)

Don't forget one-off data conversion jobs: you have the opportunity either to include them in technical complexity or to size their functionality (although if they have been built then in the authors' view it is more sensible to size them than to include them in technical complexity). Ask about *batch reports*, and ask about interfaces to other systems where data is either being sent there as the end result of a logical transaction, or where data is being received as the start of a logical transaction.

Keep an eye on the growing list of transactions. Ask yourself if they fit together or is something missing (e.g. in our case study in Chapter 3 how did the doctor details get on the system in the first place?). Are the apparent misfits or missing items part of this project, or are they accounted for by another project?

2. *Draw an entity model*

Draw an entity model and use this to check the transactions. By this stage you should have identified at least the major entities from the way that the person who is knowledgeable about the system has described it. Draw these on a sheet of paper and establish the relations between them. Try to draw out of the other person the other items of data that are required. Don't be too concerned about 100% accuracy at this stage: the model can be refined as you size the transactions in step 3.

It is extremely useful to draw the model in third normal form first time. Try to resist the idea of normalizing it later, since this only lengthens the process. Although the cardinality of the relationships doesn't matter for FPA, it is useful to get them right, since this will reveal *many to many* relationships where an entity has been missed.

When drawing the model in third normal form, keep asking whether each entity really is a separate entity as far as this system is concerned. There is a danger of generating a plethora of entities that hide the primary entities. For instance, in a system holding company accounts, a list of auditors may be stored. These could be quite adequately represented as a single entity called *auditor*. The attributes would include forename and surname. It is, however, possible to imagine a customer database where *name* is itself an entity and has associated entities of *name component* and *name component type*. Care must be taken not to over-analyse (or indeed under-analyse) the system.

At this stage, if you don't fully understand the processing, keep asking until you do: there may be more there. Quite often people are unclear because they themselves don't understand and don't want to mention the areas that they either fear they will be unable to size, or that they can't describe adequately.

3. *Size each transaction*

As you size the transactions, you have another opportunity for checking that you are at the right level, i.e. are these actually logical transactions or are they at too low or too high a level? An example would be 'are we treating the addition of an address as a separate logical transaction from adding a name, whereas we should be talking about adding a client?'. Another is 'are we talking about updating a client's status, whereas we should be talking about the client's death?'. This is a business event in its own right, if this is a life assurance system where we have to pay out when a client dies.

Throughout the three steps, listen to what the person you are working with is saying and try to spot throwaway phrases that imply other transactions. For instance, people will talk about update transactions, and somewhere in the description the phrase 'add or update' will be used. Jump on phrases like that, because *add* is separate from *update*, even if they have been physically implemented using the same screens and code.

Some general rules for identifying logical transactions

The real key to identifying logical transactions sounds simple but is actually quite hard in practice. Try to think about what is logically happening within the computer implementation. The difficulty, as mentioned earlier, is that logical transactions can either be split into multiple physical transactions or physical transactions can contain multiple logical transactions.

For the remainder of this chapter we deal with the more common situations that can arise, and these probably cover the majority of situations that you will encounter. Advice on dealing with other situations is given at the end of the chapter.

Before looking at these common situations there are, however, four general principles that apply when approaching the sizing of implemented systems:

- Bear in mind the principles of FPA and what it is trying to achieve, as well as how it achieves it.
- Think about who the user of the processing is.
- Question what the processing is supplying to them.
- Identify the points in the processing at which they can make business decisions.

5.2 COMMON SITUATIONS

The following are a selection of the more common situations that can cause problems. The examples have necessarily been described in terms of an existing system and we have therefore used, as far as possible, the Elbert Super Car front desk system that has provided previous examples. An early entity model for the system can be found in Chapter 3 should you need to refer to it. If you have started reading the book at this chapter and are therefore unfamiliar with the car hire system, you may find it useful to refer to Chapter 3, where a fuller description of the system is available.

5.2.1 A screen where different users can change different fields

Figure 5.1 shows the customer amendment screen for the Elbert Super Car front desk system. Both front desk staff and sales staff can change personal details such as name, address, and telephone number. Only sales staff can amend the special agreements.

In this example, some parts of the screen can only be used by the sales staff, while the rest can be used by both sales staff and front desk staff. This indicates that there

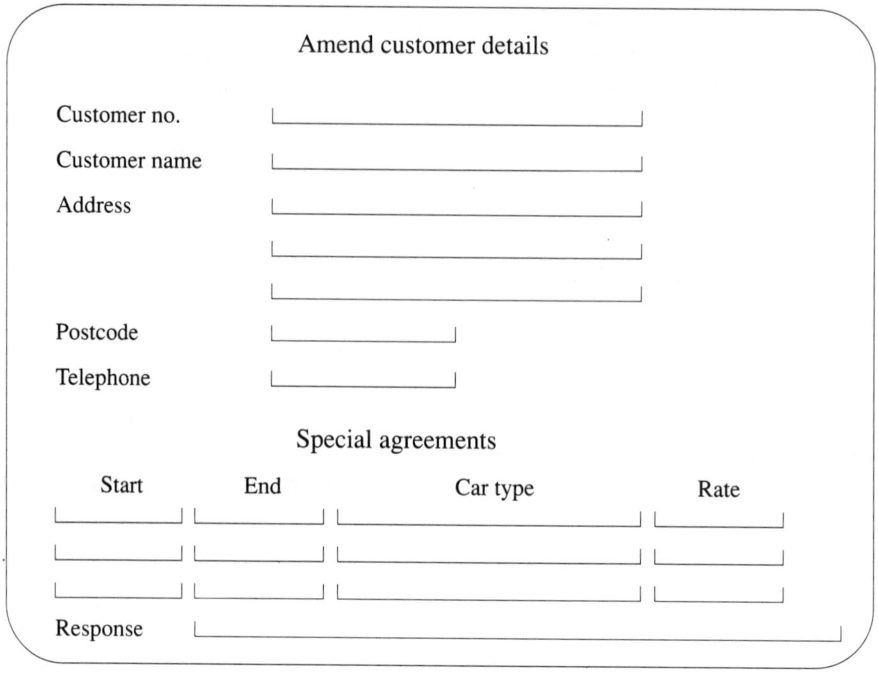

Figure 5.1 Customer amendment screen.

are at least two logical transactions. The first allows staff to amend the personal details of the customer. The second allows sales staff to amend customer agreements.

If we assume that all staff who use the transaction to amend the personal details of the customer are doing so for the same business purpose, then there are only two logical transactions. Were this not the case and the transaction was being used for different business purposes, it would be counted once for each of those business purposes.

The two logical transactions are sized as follows:

1. Amend customer personal details:
   Input   Customer no.
             Customer name
             Customer address
             Customer postcode
             Customer telephone number
   Entities Customer
   Output   Response

2. Amend customer agreement:
   Input   Customer no.
             Start date
             End date
             Car type
             Rate

Entities	Customer
	Customer agreement
Output	Response

This example raises the issue of how you deal with fields on a screen that appear to be shared by more than one logical transaction, i.e. the *customer no.* and *response* fields. If you imagine each of the transactions depicted on a data flow diagram, it would become clear that they would each have those fields separately identified as part of their data flows. Thus it can be seen that they both belong to each transaction and are therefore counted within each. It is tempting in these circumstances to count them in only one of the transactions, but this would deny any credit for performance gain from reusing code (although some might argue that the performance gain is only in the development part of the life cycle, and that there is an offsetting cost in the maintenance part of the life cycle).

When a screen, or series of screens is in front of you it is sometimes harder to spot those situations where there are multiple logical transactions on a given screen. There is no easy answer to this, except to have in the back of your mind that these situations can arise, and therefore to try to free yourself from the constraints on your thinking that are imposed by seeing physical screen layouts.

5.2.2 Menu screens

There is another situation that occurs quite frequently where more than one logical transaction uses the same screen field, and that is where data is entered on a menu screen and then used by the transaction that is subsequently selected. For instance, in Fig. 5.1 there could have been a menu screen where *customer no.* was entered, and then the user would select to either amend the personal details or amend the special agreements. *Customer no.* in this case would be what is known as *inherited input*, and would be counted as input to each of the transactions that used it. Figure 5.2 gives an example of this in the form of a *Maintain customer* menu.

This type of facility, where some information is entered and then the menu option is selected, is commonly used before update or delete transactions in order to allow details to be displayed for confirmation prior to the user updating or deleting them. This is an *enquire before* type transaction and should normally be counted as a separate enquiry. The only situation where it would not be counted as a separate enquiry is where it provides the same information as an already identified standalone enquiry.

Note that if the *enquire before update* and *enquire before delete* provide the same information they should only be counted once.

The simple rule when counting existing systems is to ask if the enquiry transactions are providing the same information, and if they are to only count them once, i.e. only count unique enquiries. If it is clear that they are being provided for different business purposes, e.g. enquire before update and enquire in order to chase outstanding debt, then count the enquiry once for each of the different business purposes.

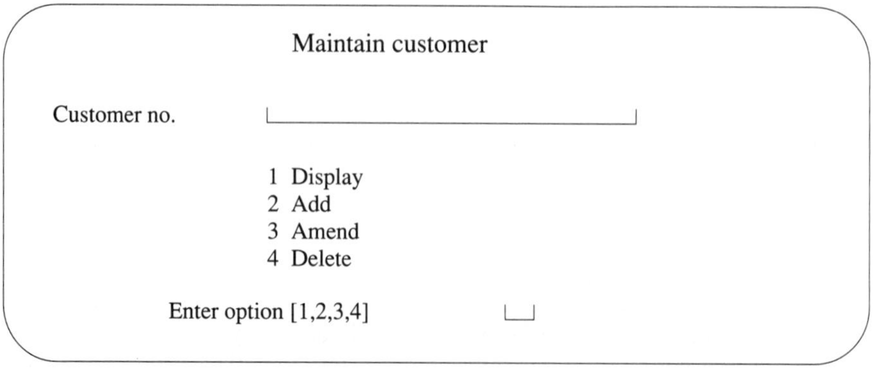

Figure 5.2 Maintain customer menu.

One final thought when considering enquiry transactions is to note that it is the information *content* and not the information *layout* that is important. If you were considering a logical design and looking at data flows you would not know the screen layout and would therefore treat two data flows with identical contents as the same data flow. Thus, features such as graphical user interfaces do not of themselves affect the system size. However, if you do come across a situation where two apparently identical data flows have a different layout, you must always question to find out if they are for different purposes, i.e. do they actually reflect two or more logical transactions? A situation where this is always the case is that of a paper copy of the information accompanying a screen copy. These outputs are produced separately and would always be produced for different reasons (commonly paper is produced to allow either a confirmation slip to be handed to a customer or to provide a paper archive, whereas the screen is there for the immediate business processing), and therefore would both be counted even if they contained identical information.

One question remains in relation to the menu screen, and that is what do we count for the screen itself? The answer is quite simply nothing. Think back to a logical model. Menus and control fields on screens would not have been represented on a logical model. They have only been introduced as a result of turning the logical model into a physical implementation; in other words they are only there for physical reasons and thus are not counted.

5.2.3 A screen that allows the user to carry out multiple functions

In Fig. 5.3, front desk staff and sales staff can add customers or change personal details such as name, address, and telephone number. Only sales staff can delete a customer or add, amend or delete the special agreements.

This is a commonly encountered implementation of the requirement to maintain customer records. This type of design optimizes project time by developing one screen that performs several functions. In this circumstance there are eight logical transactions incorporated in this screen: display, add, amend and delete both

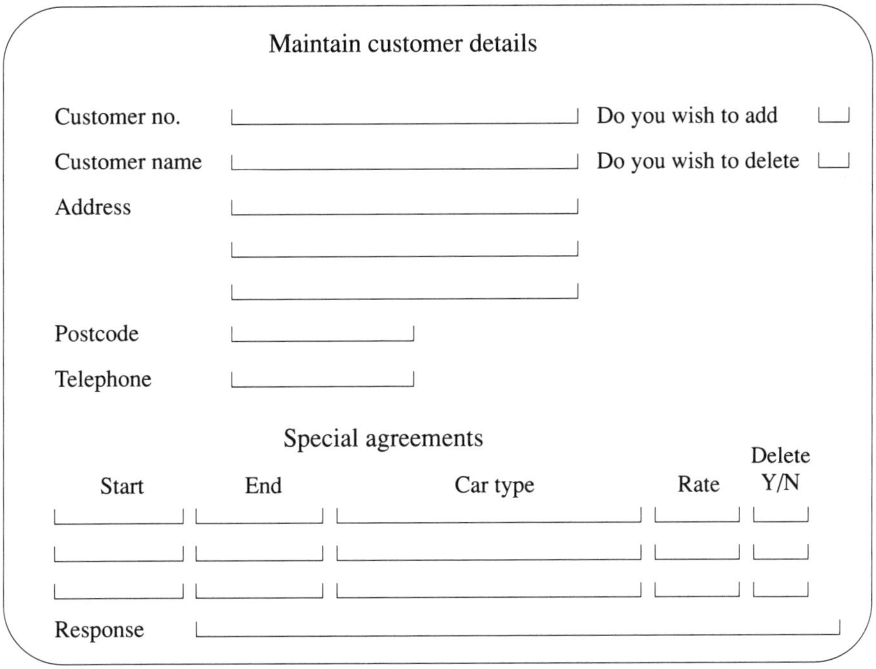

Figure 5.3 Customer maintenance screen.

customer details and customer agreements. Again, we are assuming, as with the first example, that both users are using shared transactions for the same business purpose. The eight logical transactions are sized as follows:

1. Enquire on customer
   Input   Customer no.
   Entities   Customer
   Output   Response
            Customer name
            Customer address
            Customer postcode
            Customer telephone number
2. Add customer personal details
   Input   Customer no.
            Customer name
            Customer address
            Customer postcode
            Customer telephone number
   Entities   Customer
   Output   Response
3. Amend customer personal details
   Input   Customer no.

                    Customer name
                    Customer address
                    Customer postcode
                    Customer telephone number

      Entities Customer
      Output   Response

4. Delete customer
      Input   Customer no.
      Entities Customer
                 Customer agreement
                 Hire contract
                 Car reservation
      Output   Response

5. Enquire on customer agreement
      Input   Customer no.
      Entities Customer
      Output   Response
                 Start date
                 End date
                 Car type
                 Rate

6. Add customer details
      Input   Customer no.
                 Start date
                 End date
                 Car type
                 Rate
      Entities Customer
      Output   Response

7. Amend customer agreement
      Input   Customer no.
                 Start date
                 End date
                 Car type
                 Rate
      Entities Customer
      Output   Response

8. Delete customer agreement
      Input   Customer no.
      Entities Customer
                 Customer Agreement
      Output   Response

The example illustrates some of the rules already explained above. The personal details and agreement processing are used for different business purposes and are therefore different logical transactions. Enquire, add, amend and delete offer the users different functionality.

Note that the fields that are used to allow the user to select *add* and *delete* are not counted. They are control information that is to do with the physical implementation and not the logical business system.

5.2.4 The same report is used by two users

During the design process it is often the case that similar information requirements for several users are grouped into one physical (computer) function. Figure 5.4 is an example of where this has been done for the car hire firm; both sales management and the front desk management require a report showing cars rented during a given period. The report has been produced on two-part stationery; one copy is sent to sales management to update their depot performance figures, the other copy is sent to front desk management for planning car allocation to depots.

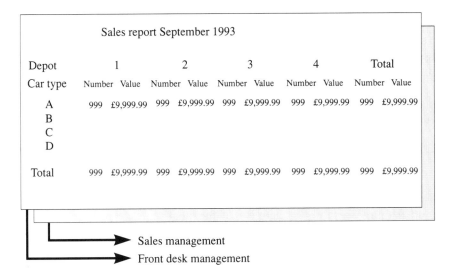

Figure 5.4 Sales report by depot and car type.

In this example there are two logical transactions. This would have been very obvious at logical system design, since two processes, each with their own separate flows, would have been shown. Each has slightly different contents, since front desk management are not interested in value (they agreed to accept a report which showed value since that reduced systems development costs).

It is often difficult to spot the fact that the information requirement of the two users is different. If the logical design is not available then it may be that further interviewing of the users involved would be the only way to realize what is going on, and this option is not always available. If in doubt, the safest option is to assume that they need the information for the same business purpose and hence to count only one logical transaction.

In the example we know what the users required, so therefore the logical transactions are:

1. Produce sales performance by district
   Input   Month end
   Entities Depot
            Car type
            Hire agreement
   Output   Car type
            Number of car rentals for a car type per depot
            Value of cars rentals for a car type per depot
            Total number of rentals for a depot
            Total value of rentals for a depot
            Total number of rentals for a car type
            Total value of rentals for a car type
            Grand total number of vehicle rentals
            Grand total value of vehicle rentals
            Date

2. Produce car movements by depot
   Input   Month end
   Entities Depot
            Car type
            Hire agreement
   Output   Car type
            Number of car rentals for a car type per depot
            Total number of rentals for a depot
            Total number of rentals for a car type
            Date

The other thing worth noting here is that the label vehicle type is variable on the report and therefore is not actually a label but is a variable field. Thus, unlike normal labels, it is counted, since it could not be pre-printed on the stationery.

5.2.5 The user can switch between unfinished tasks

This type of situation can arise in a number of different guises and can appear quite confusing. An example is given in Fig. 5.5. The example is based on the patient contact system case study in Chapter 3. In this example, due to physical limitations on screen size, the input of patient details requires two screens of information (a screen with twice as many lines would have allowed the information to be input in one screen).

In the example, each screen gives the user the option to move from one screen to the other, save the information entered, quit or complete the transaction. Each of these options is dealt with as follows:

- Move from screen to screen. In the case of moving forwards this is a device to allow the next screens of information to be entered. When moving back it is a way of reviewing what has already been entered. Neither option would exist if a bigger screen had been available, i.e. they are there simply for physical reasons – they score zero in the logical transaction count, and they do not affect the size of the

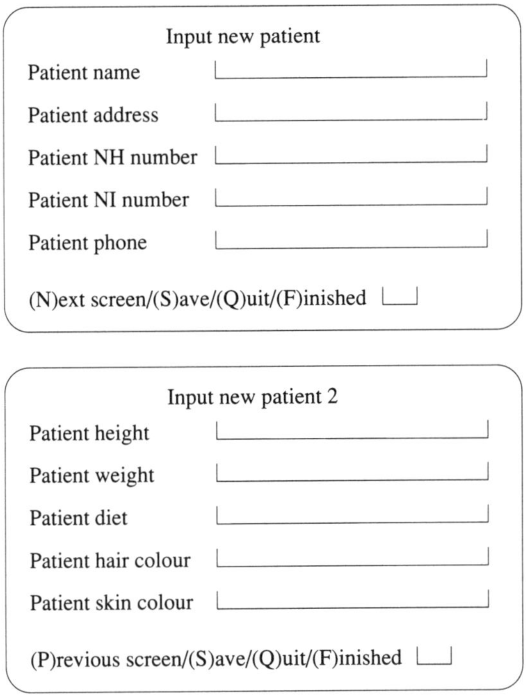

Figure 5.5 Input patient details.

logical transaction that they are part of, i.e. they do not count as input fields since they are control fields.

- Save the information entered. This option allows the user to break off in the middle of entering information, and to return to finish off at a later point. This is a bit like a clerk with several forms to complete filling in part of one and then putting it to one side until later in the day and doing something else in the meantime. This increases the usability of the system but again affects neither the number of transactions nor the size of the transaction that it is available in. This is the simplest case of the user being able to switch tasks; a fuller explanation of this follows after the remaining two options have been considered.

- Quit. The user can abort without any information being saved to any database. Again this is simply a control field, so counts for nothing.

- Finish the transaction. Here the user has completed all the fields and is ready to commit the data to the database. Similarly, this is again a control field and although it marks the completion of the logical transaction it does not affect the count.

The example of saving information entered so far is an interesting one. It is sometimes hard to see why there are no extra function points scored in these circumstances. The situation may be clearer if you consider the following two situations, both of which are different ways of implementing the same thing:

1. The user has multiple terminals available and simply leaves one mid-transaction in order to continue on one of the others, returning at some later time to finish off.
2. The user terminal can have multiple windows, e.g. on a PC running Microsoft Windows, and one window is minimized and left for a while while the user continues working in a different window, returning at some later time to finish off

The key here is that the information is not committed to the main database until the transaction is finished, i.e. it is not available as part of the information held on the system. If the partially entered information was available as part of the information held on the system, we would be looking at three transactions in this example, namely add patient, enquire before updating patient, and update patient.

The other situation where transactions are split by periods of time is where information is entered on-line and at some future point a batch update suite updates the main databases. This commonly occurs for technical reasons, for instance where overnight updates reduce the load during peak daytime on-line usage. In these cases the split is for technical reasons and not for business reasons. Thus the batch part is not counted separately from the on-line part: it is merely the processing part of the logical transaction. Purely internal flows, such as temporary files or message queues to communicate between on-line and batch processes, are not included in the count.

Identifying whether processing has been split for technical or business reasons can become confusing. In the above example, where overnight updates reduce the load during peak daytime on-line usage, there was clearly a user requirement relating to on-line response during the daytime. The split in the processing was being done in order to satisfy that, so why is this viewed as a split for technical reasons? The key to identifying the reason for the split is to ask a variation of the question, 'If infinite technical resource was available, would the processing have been split?'. In this case, the question would be, 'If more CPU resource was available and there were faster disk drives, would the processing have been split?', and the answer would have been 'No'. If there is no business requirement to split the processing then the split must be for technical reasons. The fact that the users wanted a fast on-line response, and even that they were not prepared to pay for faster hardware, does not affect the decision.

In our example there is one logical transaction and it would be sized as follows:

1. Collect patient data
    Input   Patient name
              Address
              Phone
              NH number
              NI number
              Height
              Weight
              Diet
              Hair colour
              Skin colour
    Entities Patient
    Output   Response

5.2.6 A batch program performs multiple functions

Batch suites can be hard to analyse. The easiest approach is to reduce the amount of batch analysis required by counting all the on-line functionality first. This has the advantage that all batch functionality that is simply part of a transaction split over time will have been counted. As we saw in the last example, an update or addition to the database that occurs in batch mode for purely technical reasons (e.g. building indexes on-line would degrade system performance by an unacceptable amount) are included as part of the on-line functionality used to enter the information in the first place.

This approach usually leaves a much reduced amount of processing to consider, which can then be divided into two types: periodic reporting and database changes from sources external to the system (i.e. other systems or via mechanisms, such as tape or punched card).

Periodic reporting typically includes reports that are produced overnight, e.g. daily sales, monthly commission figures or annual profits. Any other type of report produced by batch suites should have been dealt with by consideration of either on-line processing or the batch database changes from external sources. For instance, reports produced as output from updating a customer, where the clerk has input the customer details on-line and the system has updated overnight (for technical reasons), would be counted as part of that logical transaction.

Periodic reports are counted in the same way as on-line reports, i.e. they have an input (which is the time trigger that starts them, logically equivalent to the user manually selecting the report), some processing and some output. If the job picks up parameters from the job stream, for instance a date range, then these would of course count as input to the transaction.

The other type of batch processing commonly found involves changes to the database from external sources, for instance magnetic tapes. In these cases there may be a number of logical transactions in the one batch program.

If we take the example of a tape which contains customer records and order records, and for each of these the tape could contain information requiring addition of new customers and/or new orders for a customer, changes to customers' details and/or changes to customer orders, and deletions of customers and/or deletions of customer orders, then there would be six logical transactions provided by the batch program that processes the tape:

- Add customer
- Add customer order
- Amend customer details
- Amend order details
- Delete customers
- Delete order

Each logical transaction will have an input component, a processing component and an output component. The processing and output components are easy to deal with and are handled in the same way as on-line transactions, i.e. identify the entities accessed for the processing and the different field types in the outputs.

The input is slightly trickier and hinges around whether or not the incoming information has to be validated or not. If the input requires no validation and is simply written straight to the database, then it can be thought of as processed entities and the input count is one for the trigger that starts the process. If the input has to be validated, then count one for each field type in the input that is relevant to the transaction. Extra fields that it does not require and which it therefore ignores would not be included in the input count.

Figure 5.6 has an example of a batch suite that updates the vehicle master file for new rentals and produces reports summarizing updates to rental agreements and detailing vehicle availability by depot.

In this example the update report is produced as part of the processing of the updates. Had the update transaction not been split over time the report detail would have been output for each update. Since this is simply the batch part of a transaction that is split over time, we would revisit the counts for the on-line part of the system and ensure that this has been included there.

The second part of the batch process involves overnight addition of rental agreements and then the production of a daily vehicles report. In this case, the addition of rental agreements is simply the batch part of a transaction split over time, so again we would revisit the count for the on-line part and ensure that it has been included there. The report, however, is a periodic report summarizing daily rentals. Even were the other half of this process not split over time, this report would still only be produced overnight once all daily processing were complete. This is a logical transaction in its own right and should be counted as such. It would have an input (logically the day for which it is to report), it would process a number of entities, and it would have a number of output fields.

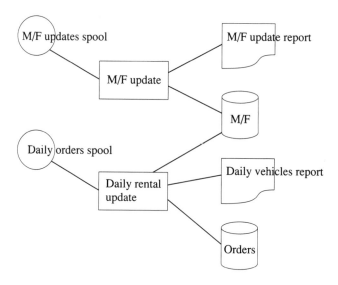

Figure 5.6 Batch update and report.

5.3 SUMMARY OF PRINCIPLES FOR DEALING WITH IMPLEMENTED SYSTEMS

This section provides a summary of the principles explained above, and some of the more immediately relevant rules from earlier chapters.

5.3.1 Count types not occurrences

In Fig. 5.1, although there are three rows for special agreement information, each containing four field types, they were counted as four field types and not as 3×4 (i.e. 12) field types. In FPA we count the number of different field types in a data flow for a logical transaction, not the number of occurrences of those field types.

This means that although the start date and end date in that example are both dates, they are different types of date and are therefore counted as two field types. However, in the case of the address there are three address lines. Because each is processed in the same way, they are counted as one field type. If they were processed differently (e.g. Street, Town, County) and subject to different validation they would be counted as three.

5.3.2 Standard headings/footings are not counted

Figure 5.3 had an example where the screen had the heading 'Maintain customer detail'; this is not giving the user business information but describing the system. It is not counted. There are two ways of looking at this which might aid understanding of this rule. The first is that standard headings etc. would not be identifiable on a logical model, since they do not give business information, or secondly that they could be supplied as pre-printed on the stationery or screen, and hence are outside the boundary of the system.

In Fig. 5.4, however, the report has a heading 'Sales Report September 1993'. Part of this is business information: it is telling the user that the report that follows is for September 1993, not October or January. The date, September 1993, is a variable field and therefore is counted as one output field.

5.3.3 Field labels, descriptors, delimiters etc. are not counted

This rule is actually just a logical expansion of the previous rule. These sorts of field are aids to the user, not business information, and are not counted. The two suggested ways of viewing the previous rule are applicable here too.

In Fig. 5.3, Customer no., Customer name etc. only describe what is in the following fields and do not add to the total system size.

These two rules could effectively be summarized as 'Do not count things that could be pre-printed'.

5.3.4 Error messages and confirmation responses are fields

In Fig. 5.1 there is an output 'Response'. This is a field that contains a message from the system to the user. Its contents are variable and are therefore counted.

If the message was of a more complex type, e.g.

Field name, Field contents, Error text

the error message would consist of three fields (see also the next rule).

5.3.5 An input field redisplayed as output is counted for both input and output

This rule only applies where the user actually wanted the input redisplayed as output. Like all other aspects of FPA, if the user does not want it then do not count it. For instance, if the user wished the information left on the screen and due to technical reasons you had to redisplay the screen, then that does not count as redisplay. Similarly, paging backwards and forwards, as in the example in Fig. 5.5, does not count as input redisplayed as output and is not counted.

In order for it to be counted, apart from the user requesting it, it is necessary that it is being displayed in a different way, e.g. flashing, highlighted or produced on a different medium. Simply passively leaving the input on the screen does not count as redisplaying it. Also, forcing a user to ask for redisplay because of technology constraints does not count either.

In a lot of error situations there is the requirement that the erroneous field is indicated. In these circumstances there is a requirement for re-outputting the information. the fields that can be highlighted should be counted for output as well as input in these circumstances.

5.3.6 Control fields, e.g. an option selection, are not counted

In both Figs 5.3 and 5.5 there are control fields, e.g.

'Do you wish to add'
'Delete Y/N'
'(N)ext screen/(S)ave/(Q)uit/(F)inish'

These supply information that control the physical implementation of the system and are not included in the count.

This rule also covers menus, which consist entirely of option selections, and are not counted at all. However, when a menu has an option selection and a field for identifying some business information, as in Fig. 5.2, it indicates that there is an input to a transaction and possibly that there is an *enquire before* type transaction.

5.3.7 Count input made in previous screens or transactions that has been carried forward into the next transaction

This is known as 'inherited input' and covers key data held over from a previous transaction that is necessary for the transaction being examined to proceed. The situation commonly arises as a result of the development team making the system more usable.

An example of this is shown in Fig. 5.1. 'Customer no.' forms part of the input for both *amend customer* and *amend customer special agreement*. In order to save the user typing, the system remembers the Customer no. as the user moves from the *amend customer* to *amend customer special agreement* transaction. In this case the input field should be counted as part of each transaction, even though it is only actually input by the user once.

Remember that it is the logical transaction that is being sized: it exists in isolation and all the data required for it to operate is counted.

5.3.8 Compound fields, if processed as a single field, count as a single field

Sometimes compound fields, such as dates (dd/mm/yy) are processed as a single field. For instance, the business is interested solely in the date and not in the day, month and year, even though a date is obviously made up of those components. An example of this might be the date on a stock report.

There are, however, situations where dates are split up and each part is separately processed, e.g. for validation. This would commonly occur on a data entry screen.

5.3.9 With arrays, count the different types of rows and columns

The number of fields = the number of row types × the number of column types. An example of this is shown in Fig. 5.4. The report is essentially an array, the elements being:

Rows

- Number of rentals by car type
- Value of rentals by car type
- Total number of rentals by car type
- Total value of rentals by car type

Columns

- Instance of each row by depot
- Total for a row across all depots

This gives eight field types, namely

- Number of car rentals for a car type per depot
- Value of car rentals for a car type per depot
- Total number of rentals for a depot
- Total value of rentals for a depot
- Total number of rentals for a car type
- Total value of rentals for a car type
- Grand total number of vehicle rentals
- Grand total value of vehicle rentals

5.3.10 Input fields with default values are treated as ordinary input fields

The default is a suggested value: the system still needs to handle whatever is input and therefore an input field is counted. No output is counted for displaying default values: this falls into the category of user help and is viewed as providing no business functionality.

5.4 COUNTING BOUGHT-IN PACKAGES

Buying a package is just another way of supplying functionality that meets users' requirements. Bought-in packages can be sized in the same way as systems written from scratch. The important thing to remember is that it is only the *required* functionality that is included in the size. All the extra bells and whistles do not add to the system size.

5.5 COUNTING TOOLS

Many IT departments supply tools that allow users to define their own facilities for reporting and data manipulation. FPA was designed primarily to measure applications and does not size tools well.

The problem with tools is that they can either be viewed as supplying infinite functionality, in that users can produce reports for any requirements they might have, or that they supply no functionality, in that the tool is, on its own and with no further effort from the user, functionless.

Internationally, function point user groups are investigating ways of extending the method to cover the sizing of tools.

All is not always lost in these circumstances. For instance, in the example of users being provided with their own facilities to produce their own reports, this is often satisfied by the system producing a flat file and the user using a commercial package to produce the reports. An approach to sizing this is to view the flat file as the output of a query, and to count the number of different field types in it and the number of entities that were accessed in order to produce it. This would then give the size of the flexible reporting part of the system, although care would have to be taken when evaluating project performance since effort may have been expended in identifying a suitable commercial package and training the users in its use, for which no credit has been given in the sizing.

5.6 CONCLUSION

Most problems in FPA arise when sizing systems retrospectively. Always remember to think logically and consider:

- Who is the user?
- What is the user doing with this part of the system?
- If there are other users doing a similar thing are they doing it at a different time or for a different reason?

If you are still unable to resolve the problem, then your local function point users' group should be able to point you to an answer that already exists for your situation, or alternatively they will consider the problem and provide you with an answer.

5.7 KEY POINTS

- Problems exist in sizing implemented systems because even though a delivered, physical system should have implemented the logical model, the description of *what* has been done is often obscured by *how* it was done. Thus, while the approach to sizing is a matter for personal choice, it must be methodical and rigorous.
- Screens providing different users with different functionality contain multiple logical transactions.
- Screens providing a user with multiple functions contain many logical transactions.
- A report shared by many users may be the output of multiple logical transactions.
- Features that improve usability do not add to the unadjusted function point count, e.g. menu screens are not counted.
- Transactions split over time for technical reasons are not counted as multiple transactions.
- Batch suites contain three main types of processing: the batch part of transactions split over time, periodic reporting, and database changes from external sources.

5.8 CASE STUDY

As with the preceding case studies, the following case study is designed to allow you to try out the techniques discussed in this chapter. They are a little artificial, since there is no system for you to refer to. You also have not lived with the system they are based on, so you do not have preconceived ideas about functionality to cloud the counting issues. Thus in some respects you may find them more difficult than real life, while in other respects they may be easier. The sample solutions are in Appendix D.

The case study follows on from the preceding case studies, and further information can be found in the case study sections of the earlier chapters. In particular the entity model in Chapter 4 should prove useful.

There are three example bits of the system. For each the task is to:

- Identify the logical transactions
- Calculate an unadjusted function point count

Having completed the task compare your answers with those in Appendix D. Where you find your answer is different, try to understand why it is different and perhaps re-read the relevant section of the chapter.

5.8.1 Exercise 1: Maintenance screen

Fig. 5.7 shows a screen that allows the practice to maintain the standard clinics that it offers.

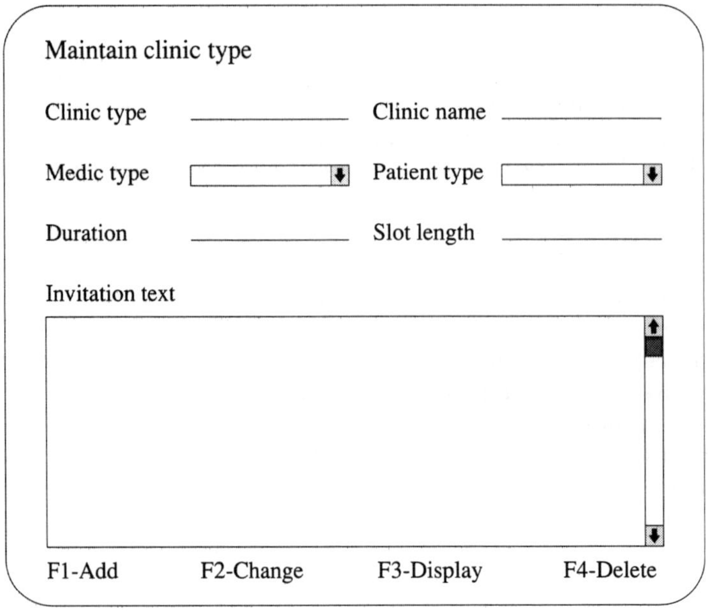

Figure 5.7 Maintain clinic type.

5.8.2 Exercise 2: Add patient

Figure 5.8 shows the two screens that must be accessed when patients are added to the system.

5.8.3 Exercise 3: Clinic report

Figure 5.9 (page 106) shows the screen used to request a report on clinic type by practitioner and the resultant report. The report is not produced instantly but instead is produced on an overnight batch run in order to avoid overloading the central database server.

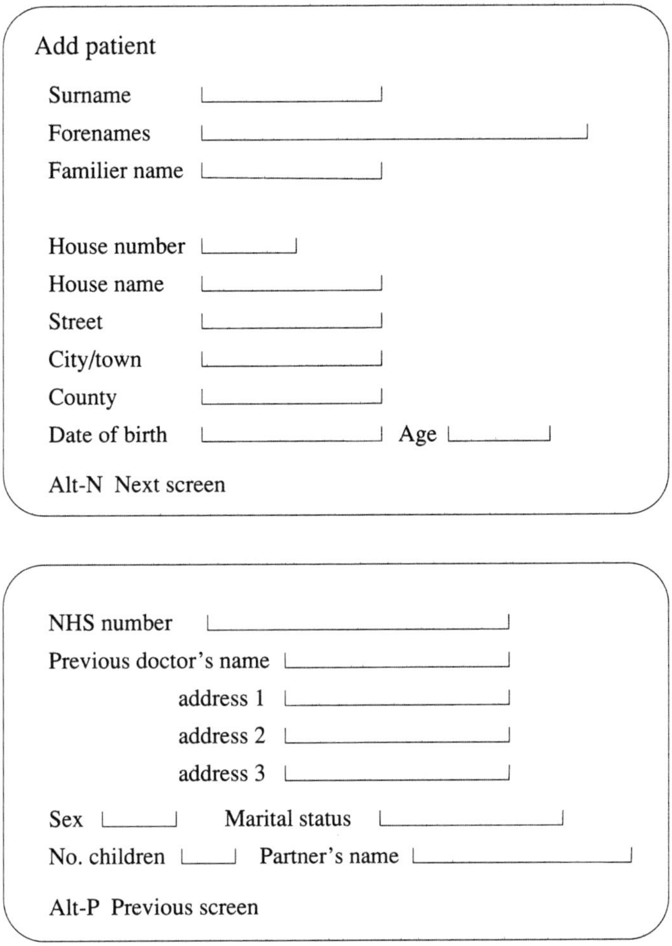

Add patient

Surname |_____|

Forenames |_____|

Familier name |_____|

House number |_____|

House name |_____|

Street |_____|

City/town |_____|

County |_____|

Date of birth |_____| Age |_____|

Alt-N Next screen

NHS number |_____|

Previous doctor's name |_____|

          address 1 |_____|

          address 2 |_____|

          address 3 |_____|

Sex |____| Marital status |_____|

No. children |___| Partner's name |_____|

Alt-P Previous screen

Figure 5.8 Add patient screens.

Clinic type by practitioner

Clinic type [_____ ⬇]

Staff name   [_____ ⬇]

Start date   [⬅ May ➡]   Year [current]
              1 2 3 4 5 6
              7 8 9 10 11 12 13
             14 15 16 17 18 19 20
             21 22 23 24 25 26 27
             28 29 30 31

End date   [⬅ May ➡]   Year [current]
              1 2 3 4 5 6
              7 8 9 10 11 12 13
             14 15 16 17 18 19 20
             21 22 23 24 25 26 27
             28 29 30 31

F1 to submit   F2 to cancel

Clinic type	Date	Number of patients	Clinic name

Figure 5.9 Report on clinic type by practitioner.

6

FUNCTION POINT COUNTING IN SYSTEMS SUPPORT

6.1 INTRODUCTION

The purpose of this chapter is to look at the practical application of FPA in the systems support environment. An approach to applying FPA will be presented together with a worked example. By the end of the chapter the reader will understand the uses and limitations of FPA in the support environment, and be able to apply FPA in practice in those situations where its use is appropriate.

6.1.1 What is systems support?

Prior to this chapter we have concentrated on applying FPA to projects involving new development, i.e. building new systems either where there were none before or where existing systems are being replaced. In practice, experience shows that a significant proportion, if not the majority of the work carried out by the average IS department, is in the supporting of systems already operating. Support work involves the following three main areas of activity:

- *Advice and assistance*: The work that is done by the support team in answering questions from the users of the systems being supported, informing them of new developments, and providing them with appropriate training.
- *Maintenance*: The work associated with ensuring system availability: fixing errors, maintaining data etc.
- *Enhancements*: The work associated with alterations to the system's functionality in response to requests from users, e.g. adding new fields to screens, removing lines from reports, storing additional information.

6.1.2 What problems are faced in support work?

A major problem faced by managers of support departments is that planning and control seem difficult if not impossible in their area. The difficulty in managing the work stems chiefly from the fact that the work tends to be event-driven. That is, work arises as a result of *ad hoc* requests rather than as an output of strategic planning.

The problems caused by the lack of planning are exacerbated by the fact that this type of work is generally of a short duration, resulting in what is commonly termed the 'fire fighting' mentality, i.e. all available resources are constantly employed tackling problems as they arise, and they rush from one problem to the next. The fact that everyone is overcommitted adds to the difficulties in controlling the work that is under way.

The problem is how to control the support operation, and to staff it in a way that is not wasteful. The first step in establishing control is to quantify what is going on, i.e. to introduce some simple measures of the work in progress. These simple measures can be supplied by the application of FPA.

6.2 APPLYING FPA IN THE SUPPORT ENVIRONMENT

FPA has a part to play in the support environment. It is of relatively limited use in the advice and assistance or maintenance areas. It is of much greater use in the enhancements area.

In considering the application of FPA in the support environment, one question that has to be addressed is 'Why would one want to use it?'. Chapter 7 is devoted to the uses of FPA and covers the topic in some detail. For the purposes of illustration we will assume that productivity measurement is the use to which we wish to put FPA. It may be useful to refer to Chapter 7 if you are unclear about productivity measurement.

6.2.1 Advice and assistance

As we have seen, FPA sizes systems by breaking them into logical transactions and then counting the components of each of those transactions. The difficulty with advice and assistance is that it does not result in any functionality being produced or changed. Thus counting function points is impossible here.

In Chapter 5 we did examine techniques for the sizing of completed systems. One of the reasons for doing so is that we can use the size of either the system or the logical transactions for which advice and assistance is being given as part of a measurement program for the support area. For instance, a metric such as:

$$\text{Effort expended per period/Size}$$

gives an aspect of the support cost per unit system that could then be compared across systems to identify training requirements, redevelopment opportunities etc.

Clearly other factors would have to be considered as well, but the above does serve to illustrate that it is possible to make sensible use of FPA in this aspect of the support area without having to learn new counting techniques.

6.2.2 Maintenance

This area of support work is principally focused on keeping the system working to specification. This mainly involves fixing defects, although it may also involve ensuring adequate disk space etc.

Defects fall into two groups, abends and functional failures. An abend type defect would be one where the system stops processing abruptly, e.g. attempting to divide by zero or closing a file that is not open. A functional failure is one where the system does not cease processing, but simply does not do the correct job, e.g. the column of numbers is not added correctly or the system does not accept input that should be valid.

Functional failures can be confusing: it is very easy to see them as enhancements. Imagine in our car hire system that the customer information screen only accepts 10 digit phone numbers. The problem for the firm is that not only are international numbers difficult to store, but since the UK has moved to 11 digit numbers no numbers can be stored. Is this enhancement or maintenance? For the purposes of this book it will be taken as maintenance, since the constraint that phone numbers will be 10 digits is not a business constraint; rather, it is imposed by the systems designer. Another way of viewing this issue is to ask whether the data flow diagram would have shown numbers as 10 digits; the answer in this case is that it would not have.

Our definition of maintenance will further include all abends and only those functional defects where the functionality does not work as the development team intended it to, based on the final agreed requirements specification.

Having defined maintenance in this way it becomes clear that the process of fixing defects results in no new functionality, merely in the correction of existing functionality. What then should be counted? Attempts to size the defect, for instance by counting how many input fields were incorrectly validated, results in meaningless numbers.

From a business perspective the measure should be the cost of the defect to the business, both in repair cost and in business impact. From an IT department view, however, there are some measures based around FPA that can be of use. These could include:

Number of defects/system size
Number of defects/logical transaction size
Effort spent on defects/size (system or transaction)

Each of these measures would help to identify problem transactions/systems. This kind of information can contribute to the prioritization process when planning redevelopment or replacement of older systems. As with the advice and assistance area, other measures would have to be taken into account. The ones suggested are intended to illustrate that FPA can be applied to this aspect of support work.

6.2.3 Enhancements

An enhancement is a user-requested change to the functionality of the system. For instance, in our car hire system there may be a requirement to include a second phone number for clients so that their daytime and evening numbers can be recorded.

The dictionary definition of enhance is *'to intensify or increase in quality etc.; improve; augment'*. In IT terms this means that an enhancement can do one or more of the following three things:

- Add functionality
- Remove functionality
- Change functionality

An enhancement can affect both the information processing requirements of a system, and its technical requirements.

In the case of a change to the information processing requirements, because an enhancement is altering functionality it affects logical transactions. It may be that a single enhancement affects many logical transactions; taking the phone number example, the add, update and display transactions will be changed as a result of storing two phone numbers for a customer instead of one. These changes to logical transactions are the key to sizing enhancements.

In the case where the enhancement involves a change to the technical requirements of the system the change to the TCA could be measured, but see the discussion on TCA in Chapter 2 when considering the merits of this approach.

Changes to requirements can also be required during the normal systems development life cycle prior to implementation of a system under development. These are usually called change requests. The sizing techniques discussed here for enhancements would be equally applicable to change requests.

What measures are appropriate for enhancements?

Bearing in mind the fact that enhancements result in one or more of functionality being added, removed or changed, there are two basic types of measure that can be made:

- The system size before and after the enhancement
- The size of the enhancement being made

These types of measure can be broken down into the following:

FPI_o = Size of the system before enhancement
FPI_n = Size of the system after enhancement
FPI_e = Size of the enhancement
FPI_a = Size of added functionality
FPI_d = Size of deleted functionality
FPI_c = Size of changed functionality

Note: UFP$_o$ is the unadjusted function point size of the system before enhancement. Similarly, each of UFP$_n$, UFP$_e$, UFP$_a$, UFP$_d$, and UFP$_c$ are the unadjusted function point sizes for the corresponding FPI term.

The authors' experience is that in many cases it is simply not useful to collect each of FPI$_a$, FPI$_d$ and FPI$_c$ individually. Instead, the size of the enhancement (FPI$_e$) is used. It is calculated as:

$$FPI_e = FPI_a + FPI_d + FPI_c$$

Each of these measures allows a productivity figure to be calculated using the standard format of:

$$Productivity = Size/Effort$$

There are arguments for and against using the FPI$_e$ simplification. Relying on it requires one to make one of two assumptions: either that the productivities of adding, deleting and changing functionality are similar, or that the relative proportions of addition, deletion and change across projects remain roughly constant.

The approach to take is best decided by consideration of what information you need and how you are going to use it. If your aim is to calculate productivity figures, then in using FPI$_a$, FPI$_c$, and FPI$_d$ you must consider whether or not effort figures are available for each of the types of work. In many projects it is often hard enough to produce reasonable figures for the split between new development components and enhancement components, without trying to split enhancements further into addition, deletion and change.

For the purposes of this chapter we shall assume that we wish to identify FPI$_a$, FPI$_d$ and FPI$_c$ separately. We shall also calculate FPI$_e$ for illustration.

Steps to sizing enhancements

There are 11 steps to sizing an enhancement. These are listed below, and then each one is considered in turn in conjunction with a worked example from the car hire system.

1. Identify the logical transactions affected.
2. For each transaction, count:

   - Input fields, entities and output fields added
   - Input fields, entities and output fields removed
   - Input fields, entities and output fields handled differently

3. Calculate totals for all added input fields, entities and output fields.
4. Calculate totals for all removed input fields, entities and output fields.
5. Calculate totals for all input fields, entities and output fields handled differently.
6. Calculate totals for all affected input fields, entities and output fields (i.e. added + removed + handled differently).
7. For each set of totals, calculate the unadjusted function points using the standard formulae given in Chapter 2. In summary they are:

$$\text{UFP} = N_i \times W_i + N_{er} \times W_{er} + N_o \times W_o$$

8. Recalculate the TCA for the system.
9. Calculate each of FPI_a, FPI_d, FPI_c, and FPI_e by multiplying the relevant UFP by the TCA.
10. Adjust the old system size (UFP_o) by adding UFP_a and subtracting UFP_d to give the new system size (UFP_n).
11. Calculate the new function point index (FPI_n) by multiplying UFP_n by the new TCA.

Introduction to the worked example

The worked example is taken from Elbert Super Car's front desk system which we have used in previous chapters, and concerns the reservation maintenance screen. The screen layout is shown in Fig. 6.1. To use the screen, a customer code is input by the front desk clerk, the system responds by displaying the customer's name and the latest reservation, if any, for that customer. The clerk can then input a new reservation, change the details of the reservation or delete it.

The data flow diagram for the screen is shown in Fig. 6.2.

Elbert Super Car have provided a list of changes that they would like made to the system, these are shown in Fig. 6.3.

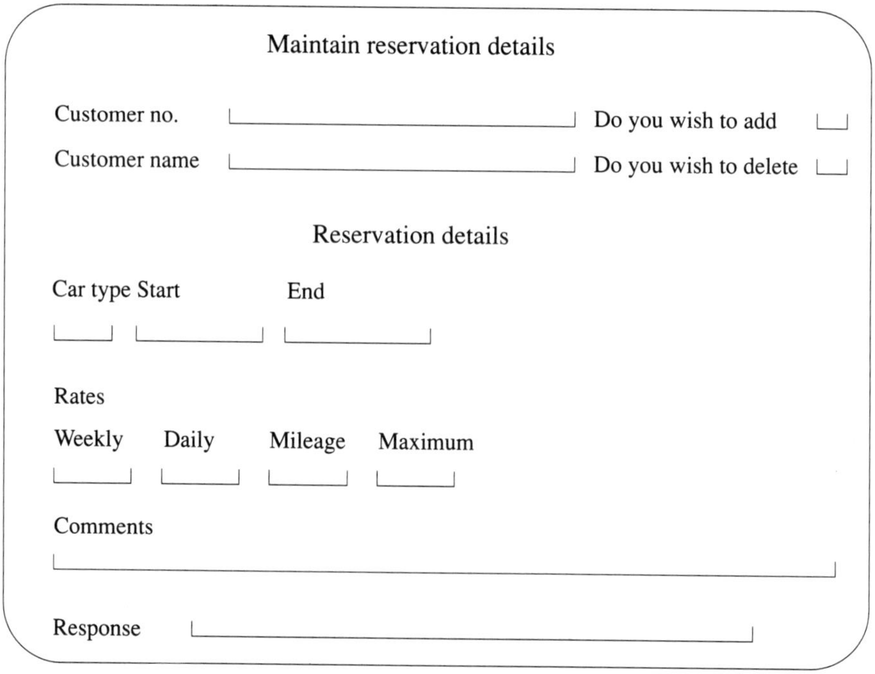

Figure 6.1 Reservation maintenance screen.

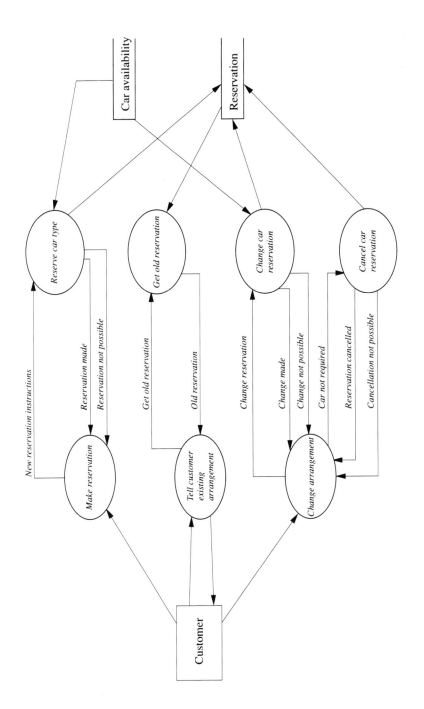

Figure 6.2 Reservation maintenance DFD.

113

Potential changes to reservations

1. At present the system only allow one reservation per customer. It needs to be enhanced to allow up to 99 reservations per customer.
2. The system needs to allow 'N/A' in the Maximum charge field.
3. When a reservation is deleted a comment giving the reason must be collected and a record made of the cancelled reservation. These cancelled reservations must be reported upon monthly and archived.
4. The user no longer requires the customer name to be displayed.

Figure 6.3 Potential changes to the reservation maintenance part of the system.

For this worked example, we shall estimate the size of the enhancement by examining which size components (e.g. fields and entities) are affected. We shall then calculate the relevant UFP and FPI figures.

Had we been sizing the enhancements after implementation the process would have been no different, except that we would have known what the impact was as opposed to estimating it.

One source of confusion at this stage will be understanding the impact of the enhancements listed in Fig. 6.3. In order to ensure that this does not cloud the explanation of counting the enhancements, the next four sections are devoted to explaining the impact of each enhancement in a little more detail.

Worked example: overview of change 1

The requirement to allow each customer to have multiple reservations will impact each of the options on the screen. It is probable that the reservations entity would have an attribute called *reservation no.* added, so that the customer and Elbert Super Car could refer easily to any particular reservation. Thus each screen option will require either to display the reservation number in enquiry screens, or to accept as input the reservation number in the add reservation screen (or perhaps to display an automatically incremented reservation number).

There is a difficulty in deciding whether this example is an enhancement or whether it is actually maintenance. It could be that a limit of one reservation was a design error or a deliberate design limitation. The user may even have agreed at design time that customers never have more than one reservation. In this case it would be maintenance. On the other hand, the business could have had rules that explicitly prevented a customer from making more than one reservation. In these circumstances it would be valid to call this an enhancement.

Worked example: overview of change 2

The ability to accept N/A as the maximum charge is simply allowing another value for maximum charge. The maximum charge is already stored on an entity so no change is logically required to the entity. It may be that physically the relevant attribute of the entity is defined as numeric. In these circumstances the characters N/A could not be stored. This is a physical consideration and not a feature of the logical design. It therefore does not affect the sizing of the enhancement. This is not as unreasonable as it seems, since it would probably be implemented by storing zero (or a very large number) as the maximum charge. This maintains the attribute as numeric on the entity.

The only change we need to consider is to the add and update screens, where the user-specified validation rules for the maximum charge field do not currently allow the clerk to key N/A as input.

Worked example: overview of change 3

Storing cancelled reservations instead of simply deleting them requires a fundamental change to the delete function. A cancelled reservation requires different data stored about it from a live reservation, and it also requires different processing. For instance, the garage manager would not expect to find a cancelled reservation on the list of cars to be prepared. Thus the reservation entity is now viewed as comprising two subentities: live reservation and cancelled reservation.

The live reservation subentity is effectively the old reservation entity, and thus no change is needed to the add, display and update options, assuming that once cancelled a reservation can no longer be accessed. Thus the only change is to the delete reservation option, which will require both subentities to be processed. A new transaction to produce monthly reports of cancelled reservations will also be required.

Worked example: overview of change 4

The display option is the only one that would be affected by the user no longer requiring the customer name to be displayed.

In the add option, the customer name was an optional means of identifying the customer if the customer number was not known. This is not being changed. Similar reasoning applies to the update and delete functions.

Step 1: Identify the logical transactions affected

Any change to a system affects the physical implementation of a logical system. It is the logical aspect that is measured in FPA, so therefore the logical transactions need to be identified. The process of identification is the same as that which takes place when sizing existing systems. Chapter 5 explains the process in detail.

Referring to Figs 6.1 and 6.2, and applying the techniques discussed in Chapter 5, it can be deduced that there are currently four logical transactions. These are:

- Add reservation
- Display reservation
- Update reservation
- Delete reservation

In the discussion above, where each change request was explained, the impact on each screen option was considered. From this we can produce the following summary:

Change number	*Transactions affected*
1	All four
2	Add and update
3	Delete, plus one new transaction
4	Display

Step 2: Part 1 – counting fields and entities added

Here we are concerned with identifying fields and entities that are new to each transaction. They may be entirely new to the whole system, or they may already be in use elsewhere and are simply being included in additional transactions. In either case they are counted in the same way.

As with counting a new development, we deal with each logical transaction separately. We could of course deal with each change separately as well, if so required. For the purposes of the worked example, we shall assume that the user wants all four changes. Thus, while the working for step 1 will require us to consider the impact of each change separately, we shall only produce function point counts on the basis of the sum of the four changes. This simplifies the explanation of subsequent steps since we only have to carry one set of totals instead of four.

Change 1 requires a new reservation number field. While this requires a new attribute on the reservation entity, this does not constitute a new entity, and instead is counted as an entity processed differently. The revised layout for the Maintain reservation details screen is shown in Fig. 6.4.

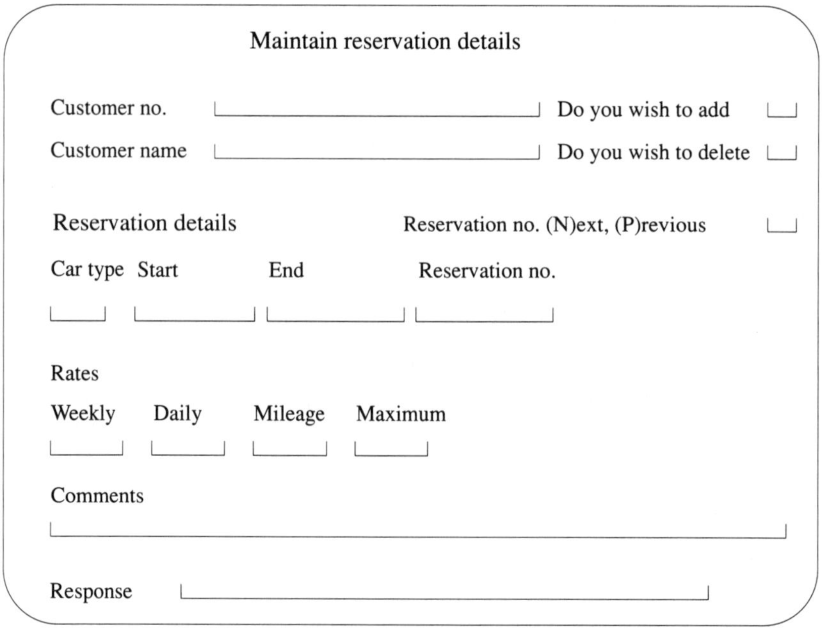

Figure 6.4 Reservation screen allowing many reservations for a customer.

Change 2 requires no additions.

Change 3 requires a new comment field for cancelled reservations as well as a new *cancelled reservation* entity. It additionally requires a new transaction to report on cancelled reservations on a monthly basis. The layout for this report is shown in Fig. 6.5.

Reservations cancelled (*Month***)**				
Customer	**Car type**	**Start**	**End**	**Value**
(Customer name)	*(Car type description)*	*(Date)*	*(Date)*	*99999.99*
Reason				
(Comment . . . .)				
"	"	"	"	"
"	"	"	"	"
Total value for customer "	"	"	"	999999.99
Customer	**Car type**	**Start**	**End**	**Value**
(Customer name)	*(Car type description)*	*(Date)*	*(Date)*	*99999.99*
Reason				
(Comment . . . .)				
"	"	"	"	"
"	"	"	"	"
Total value for customer "	"	"	"	999999.99
Total value cancelled				999999.99

Figure 6.5 Monthly cancelled reservations report.

Looking at Fig. 6.5, we need to count an input to trigger the monthly report, output fields for each of the report fields (these are identified in parentheses in Fig. 6.5), and entities to extract the information from. The entities will be Customer (for customer name), Car type (for car type description), Reservation (for the total value for customer) and Cancelled reservation for the remainder.

Change 4 requires no new additions.

Thus we can produce the following summary for added functionality:

Transaction	*Input fields*	*Entities*	*Output fields*
Enquire	Reservation No.		Reservation No.
Add	Reservation No.		
Amend	Reservation No.		
Delete	Reservation No.	Cancelled reservation	
	Comment		
Produce cancelled reservation report	Time trigger	Customer reservation	Month
		Car type	Customer name
		Cancelled reservation	Car type description
			Comment
			Start date

Table continued

Transaction	Input fields	Entities	Output fields
			End date
			Value
			Total value
			customer
			Total value
			cancelled

Step 2: Part 2 – counting fields and entities removed

Here we are concerned with identifying those fields and entities no longer required in each logical transaction. It may be that they are being removed from the whole system, or simply from a few transactions. It makes no difference to counting, since the approach is to count each logical transaction separately.

Only change 4 involves the removal of functionality: the customer name will no longer be displayed.

Transaction	Input fields	Entities	Output fields
Enquiry			Customer name

Step 2: Part 3 – counting fields and entities handled differently

When counting fields and entities handled differently we are identifying functionality that already exists but which is being altered. In the case of input fields we are looking for changes to the format or validation of the field. For output fields we are looking for changes to the positioning or format of the field. For entities we are looking for additional or removed attributes.

Change 1, as we saw earlier, involves an alteration to the reservations entity. A new attribute, *reservation no*, is being stored on the entity. Change 2 requires the validation of the field *maximum value* to be changed. Neither change 3 nor change 4 involves any fields or entities handled differently. Thus we can produce the following summary for functionality handled differently:

Transaction	Input fields	Entities	Output fields
Enquire		Reservation	
Add	Maximum value	Reservation	
Amend	Maximum value	Reservation	
Delete		Reservation	

Step 3: Total all added fields and entities

Totalling the above gives:

Input fields	Entities	Output fields
6	5	10

Step 4: Total all removed fields and entities

Totalling the above gives:

Input fields	Entities	Output fields
0	0	1

Step 5: Total all differently handled fields and entities

Totalling the above gives:

Input fields	Entities	Output fields
2	4	0

Step 6: Produce a total for all affected inputs, processed entities and outputs

This step produces an input, process, output size that will be used to calculate FPI_e. Totalling the above gives:

Input fields	Entities	Output fields
8	9	11

Step 7: Multiply by the appropriate set of weights for this system

$$UFP_a = (6 \times 0.58) + (5 \times 1.66) + (10 \times 0.26) = 14.38$$
$$UFP_d = (0 \times 0.58) + (0 \times 1.66) + (1 \times 0.26) = 0.26$$
$$UFP_c = (2 \times 0.58) + (4 \times 1.66) + (0 \times 0.26) = 7.80$$
$$UFP_e = (8 \times 0.58) + (9 \times 1.66) + (11 \times 0.26) = 22.44$$

Step 8: Recalculate the TCA for the system

Sometimes a change request can be made that may not change the information processing requirements of the system, but will alter the technical requirements of the system, e.g. to improve response times. In these circumstances the TCA may need to be recalculated, depending on what you are using the function point data for.

If you are looking at function points to analyse development projects, then post-implementation changes in environment or technical requirements do not affect the original development. If you are keeping track of size for maintenance purposes, then there may be value in recalculating the TCA. The important thing is to decide what you are trying to achieve and then to decide whether you need to recalculate the TCA.

The changes in the worked example do not involve any alteration to the technical requirements of the car hire system. Thus we do not need to recalculate the TCA. Had we done so, we would have used the standard rules for calculating TCA as discussed in Chapter 2.

Step 9: Multiply by the TCA for the system.

This step gives FPI_e, i.e. the total size of the change. The TCA was calculated in the worked example in Chapter 4 as 0.83; thus:

$$FPI_e = 22.44 \times 0.83 = 18.63 \text{ fpts}$$

Step 10: Adjust the system size

In this step the size of the old system is adjusted by adding UFP_a and subtracting UFP_d to give the new system size.

If it is assumed that the original size of the system was 385 UFPs the new size is

$$385 + 14.38 - 0.26 = 399.12 \text{ UFPs}$$

Step 11: Calculate the new system size, FPI_n.

$$FPI_n = 399.12 \times 0.83 = 331$$

Summary of worked example

Using the worked example, we have seen how a change request can be analysed and a set of function point indices calculated. The use that these numbers are put to will depend on your own organization.

It is the authors' experience that FPI_e is useful in estimating, and in a controlled environment UFP_a and UFP_d can be used to track system size through the development and subsequent parts of a project life cycle. It is always worth producing a fresh count at implementation in order to ensure that an accurate system size figure is taken forward into the support area.

6.2.4 Tracking system size through the life cycle

During development a system may be counted 3 or 4 times, and then the complete system will be sized. Changes and enhancements between counts should be fewer than in the support environment; thus the continual monitoring of system size is often not necessary. There are two obvious exceptions to this: prototyping and scope creep. In prototyping the system definition is continuously evolving and thus more frequent counts are required. In scope creep, the system is subject to a number of change requests which expand the scope of the original project; again, more frequent counts are required.

While a system is being supported, however, it is in a constant state of flux requiring frequent 'snapshots' of system and support product size. This means that a change sizing worksheet and a system monitoring worksheet will be useful. Figure 6.6 shows a change sizing worksheet for change 1 from our worked example. This sample worksheet has space to identify the system, the area of the system and the change concerned. There are then three sections for the types of work performed:

Functionality added
Functionality removed
Functionality changed

Change sizing worksheet

SYSTEM: *Car hire*

SYSTEM AREA: *Reservations*

CHANGE No. 1 CHANGE DESCRIPTION: *Allow 99 reservations per customer*

Functionality added

Transaction	Input	Entities	Output
Enquire	1		1
Add	1		
Amend	1		
Delete	1		
Total added	4		1

Functionality removed

Transaction	Input	Entities	Output
Total removed			

Functionality changed

Transaction	Input	Entities	Output
Enquire		1	
Add		1	
Amend		1	
Delete		1	
Total changed		4	
Total handled	4	4	1

Figure 6.6 Example change sizing worksheet.

Within these sections the transactions affected are identified and the number of input fields, entities and output fields worked on is shown. Each section is totalled and a grand total for all components affected by the change is given. This document, completed for each change, could prove valuable for auditing and for detailed analysis of support performance.

It is useful to have a system size monitoring worksheet which gives a summary of the statistics collected for analysis on a periodic basis. Figure 6.7 gives an example for the car hire system.

The columns shown in Fig. 6.7 have the following meanings:

1. Period end: Date of end of support management accounting period.
2. Start UFPs: Unadjusted function point size at start of period
3. UFPs added: Number of unadjusted function points added during period
4. UFPs rem.: Number of unadjusted function points removed during period
5. UFPs chnged: Number of unadjusted function points altered during period
6. UFPs hndld: Column 3 + Column 4 + Column 5

System size monitoring worksheet

System:..

Period end	Start UFPs	UFPs added	UFPs rem.	UFPs chnged	UFPs hndld	End UFPs	Start TCA	End TCA	Start FPI	End FPI	Hndld FPI	No. changes	Work hours
31/10	385	14.12	0.26	7.8	22.18	398.86	0.835	0.835	321.475	333.048	18.52	4	200

Figure 6.7 Example change system size monitoring worksheet.

7. End UFPs: Column 2 + Column 3 − Column 4
8. Start TCA: TCA at start of period
9. End TCA: TCA at end of period
10. Start FPI: Column 2 × Column 8
11. End FPI: Column 7 × Column 9
12. Handld FPI: Column 6 × Column 9
13. No. changes: Number of change requests implemented during period
14. Work hours: Effort expended on enhancements during period

6.3 CONCLUSION

It is both possible and valuable to produce function point counts for support activities. The figures suggested above would be an excellent starting point, but different installations will find that they need to consider which figures are relevant to them.

6.4 KEY POINTS

- Support work consists of advice and assistance, maintenance and enhancements.
- Function point analysis is applied to the systems support area to provide measurements that bring more objective control to the support function.
- A range of size measures are available but their practicality needs to be considered for each organization.
- Counting techniques are a mix of skills gained in the previous chapters.

6.5 CASE STUDY

For general notes on case studies, please refer to the introductory text in the case study of Chapter 2.

Each of the components of this case study comprises a change request detailing changes required to the screens/reports used in the Chapter 5 case study. For ease of reference the screens are reproduced alongside the text of the change requests; however, fuller details of the logical transactions underlying the screens are available in the Chapter 5 case study as well as the solutions in Appendix D. Solutions to this case study are in Appendix E.

6.5.1 Exercise 1

Figure 6.8 shows the screen used by the practice to add new patients. With the growth of preventive medicine and active management of patient health, the practice is establishing a growing number of clinics to which it invites patients in the appropriate target group. The normal method of inviting patients is to mail a letter to them detailing the clinic and offering them an appointment. The number of letters being sent on an annual basis is such that the Royal Mail has advised the practice that if it pre-sorts its letters by postcode, it will enjoy a discount on the costs of mailing.

Please provide an estimate of the change in function point size of the transaction(s) represented in Fig. 6.8, and also the final size of the transaction after the change has been made.

6.5.2 Exercise 2

The practice administrator finds it infuriating to be required to type in both the date of birth and age of new patients. The feature was originally incorporated so that any keying errors by the administrator could be caught when the two were compared. In practice, this has not been helpful and the practice would now like to have the age field removed from the screen. Figure 6.8 depicts the screen before the change.

As with the first exercise, please provide an estimate of the change in function point size of the transaction(s) represented in Fig. 6.8, and also the final size of the transaction after the change has been made.

6.5.3 Exercise 3

Figure 6.9 shows the 'Clinic type by practitioner' report. The practice require two changes to be made to this report. The first is to sort the report into alphabetic order of practitioner. The second is optionally to limit the report to include only those clinics where clinic time represents more than 10% of the weekly actual workload of the practitioner involved.

For each of the changes please provide an estimate of the size of the change in function points, and the final size of the transaction after the change has been made.

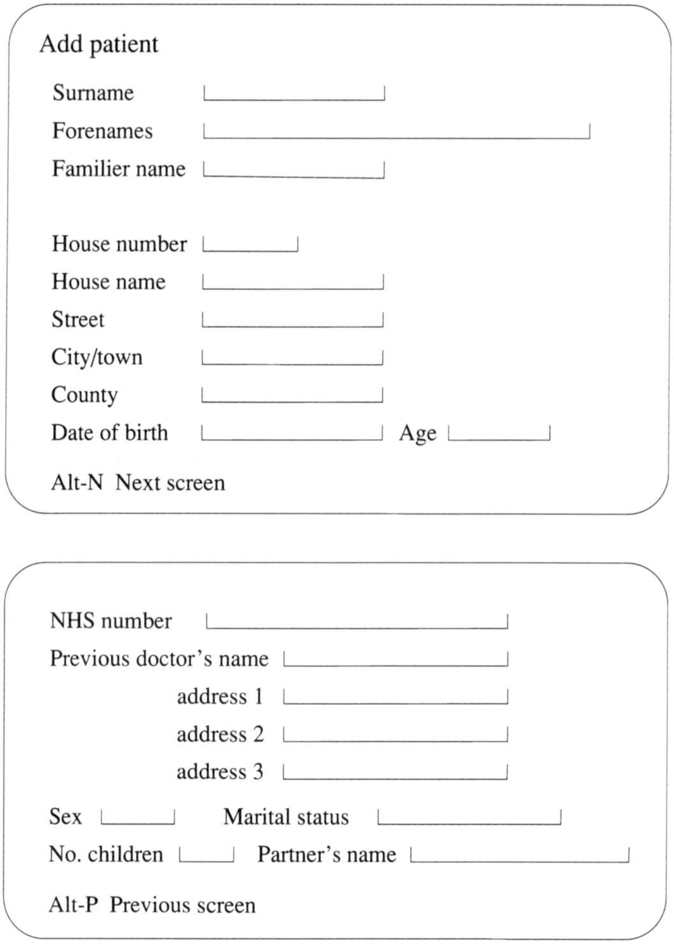

Add patient

    Surname |_____|

    Forenames |_____|

    Familier name |_____|

    House number |_____|

    House name |_____|

    Street |_____|

    City/town |_____|

    County |_____|

    Date of birth |_____| Age |_____|

    Alt-N Next screen

    NHS number |_____|

    Previous doctor's name |_____|

                address 1 |_____|

                address 2 |_____|

                address 3 |_____|

    Sex |_____| Marital status |_____|

    No. children |_____| Partner's name |_____|

    Alt-P Previous screen

Figure 6.8 Add patient screens.

6.5.4 Exercise 4

The report depicted in Fig. 6.9 is used by the practice manager to ensure a balanced workload for the medical staff in the practice. The receptionist is responsible for greeting patients and identifying those who have failed to show. The practice therefore requires that the clinic type by practitioner report is added to the receptionist's menu.

    Please estimate the impact that this will have on the function point size of the system.

Clinic type by practitioner

Clinic name [_____ ⬇]

Staff name [_____ ⬇]

Start date   [⬅   May   ➡]   Year [current]
               1 2 3 4 5 6
               7 8 9 10 11 12 13
              14 15 16 17 18 19 20
              21 22 23 24 25 26 27
              28 29 30 31

End date   [⬅   May   ➡]   Year [current]
               1 2 3 4 5 6
               7 8 9 10 11 12 13
              14 15 16 17 18 19 20
              21 22 23 24 25 26 27
              28 29 30 31

F1 to submit   F2 to cancel

Clinic type	Practitioner	Date	Number of patients	Clinic name

Figure 6.9 Clinic type by practitioner report.

7

USING FUNCTION POINTS

7.1 INTRODUCTION

The purpose of this chapter is to look at the practical use that can be made of FPA. Knowing the size of a system may for some be very interesting, but is on its own of little benefit. The practical applications of FPA considered in this chapter are Information Systems (IS) process performance measurement, IS process improvement and software development cost estimation. The calibration of the MKII estimating method is overviewed. By the end of the chapter the reader will have a basic understanding of IS process metrics and be able to produce estimates for software development given a function point index.

The arguments for establishing measures were presented in Chapters 1 and 2. Other chapters have also made reference to measures in order to illustrate, or provide a context for, aspects of FPA. In this chapter we are going to look at the basic steps involved in establishing a programme of measurement, examine the types of measurement that are available, and look at the context in which measurement takes place. This is not, however, a textbook on IT metrics collection, and as such we shall only be examining the subject in outline. It is not intended that this chapter could be the sole basis on which a metrics programme is established, since that would require a book in itself.

7.2 BASIC STEPS IN ESTABLISHING A METRICS PROGRAMME

There are various approaches that can be taken to the establishment of a metrics programme, and there are many textbooks on the subject. The approach outlined here is one way of doing it that has been successfully applied in a number of organizations. The reader is recommended to research the subject in more depth before embarking on a metrics programme.

7.2.1 GQM

The basis of the approach is a technique known as GQM, or goal, question, metric. Various authors have written about the technique (some examples are Paul Goodman (1994) and Norman Fenton (1991)). The idea is that the organization establishes some goals, then derives some questions that must be answered to determine whether the goal is being met, and finally establishes some metrics which quantify the answers to the questions. For instance:

Goal: Double productivity over 5 years
Question: What is current productivity level?
Metric: Function points/work hour

This example goal would be appropriate if the organization was looking to set IS process performance improvement targets. There are of course other reasons for establishing a metrics programme. Three other common strategies that IS departments may adopt are:

Determination of methods, tools and techniques to be used
Prioritizing projects
Planning manning levels

It is worth a brief examination of each of the strategies in order to provide a context for the basic measures that we shall be looking at later.

7.2.2 Improvement targets

In a competitive market-place, an underlying theme adopted by companies is one of continuous improvement, i.e. a constant process of becoming 'better' at supplying the customer with what is required. For IT departments the customer is the business organization as a whole and improvement can be described as 'Reliably supplying more of the customer's requirements for a given cost and timescale'. In short, improve performance. As we will see with the other strategies, 'performance' is a term that we keep using. What is meant by performance is explained in Section 7.3 which examines basic measures.

Once measurement of performance is under way and improvements are being made, there is often a desire to compare one department's (or organization's) performance against another. The introduction of objective performance figures would appear to be a vehicle for doing this. The situation is frequently not that simple. Because department A has higher performance figures than B does not necessarily mean that it is better. For instance, department A may have tools which should make them highly productive, while B is stuck in an environment where productivity-enhancing tools cannot be used. It is important therefore that the numbers are not simply compared, rather that analysis of the differences is carried out and trends compared. The same is true when comparing performance between different companies. There is an additional problem in comparing companies which does not usually exist when comparing departments, which is that the companies may be collecting the performance figures in a different way. For instance, one company's person-day or person-month may be of a different duration to another's.

One solution would be only to compare the rate of improvement, e.g. Organization A has improved productivity by 20% whereas B has improved by 10%. If they have not changed their methods of data collection it can be said that Organization A has improved more rapidly than B. There may still be problems with this approach of course. For example, in very rare cases B may be operating close to peak performance for the environment in which both organizations are operating, and therefore has less room for improvement.

7.2.3 Methods, tools and techniques to be used

The information collected from a metrics programme will give details of projects and how they have performed. Analysis of the data can identify which areas give high and which give low performance. In order to understand the differences in performance, it is essential to collect data on the environmental factors associated with each project. This is the starting point for investigations into why the differences occur between projects.

For instance, it may be noted that projects which use a new tool have lower productivity than projects which do not, despite the tool having been purchased to improve productivity. This may well be because of lack of technical staff familiarity with the tool, and improvements may come at a later stage. Conversely, a team working in a low-level language on a particularly difficult problem may produce high performance – not because of the tools used but because they are highly motivated. If the project's environmental factors are not adequately considered, incorrect conclusions may be drawn in these sorts of circumstances.

Those involved in interpreting and publishing performance information/analysis must realize that though the data will show differences in performance and may indicate potential reasons for it, the need for careful thought is not eliminated.

Information on performance derived from a metrics programme allows the following steps to be taken:

1. Establish the causes of differences between projects
2. Expand and migrate to other projects the performance improving factors
3. Reduce the detrimental factors across all projects

Use of metrics derived from analysing the effects of methods, tools and techniques will allow estimates of how much performance can be improved. This will of course be a contributor to a performance improvement strategy.

7.2.4 Priority of projects

Measurement of current performance and analysis of factors impacting performance allows projections to be made for future performance. Once projections of future performance are available, plans for the future production of systems can be prepared. In the absence of projections of future performance, the current performance could be assumed.

The first step would be to estimate rough sizes of the systems to be produced. Next, the projections of future performance can be applied to generate cost and duration estimates. Estimates of the benefits of the introduction of the new systems can be derived using traditional techniques. Armed with these data, a strategy could be to prioritize the systems according to their benefit/cost ratio: the higher the ratio the higher the priority, and hence the sooner the system would be tackled, although care would have to be taken when considering infrastructure projects.

These steps would only be a starting point: other factors, such as business plans and priorities, would obviously have to be taken into account.

7.2.5 Staffing levels

Planning future staffing levels could be done in a number of ways. If metrics were being collected such that the strategies outlined above were under way, then a timetable could be established showing:

- The sequence of projects
- Their cost and duration
- The introduction of new tools, techniques and methods

From these it may be possible to generate a schedule showing how the staffing requirements will be met. This could include:

- Number of people required
- Skills required
- Training
- Recruitment

7.2.6 The starting point

Something that is frequently overlooked is the necessity to establish the current position before goals can be set. It is necessary to produce a benchmark as a measurement baseline and thus to quantify the current process performance before setting the goals for a metrics programme.

A significant number of companies initiate metrics programmes which die a quick death. There are undoubtedly many factors that contribute to this, but among the key factors will be:

- No goals: the organization was measuring for the sake of measurement.
- Payback period, i.e. how long will it be before the programme generates benefit?
- Over-measurement, i.e. attempting to measure too much and thus causing the programme to be both expensive to the organization and onerous to those required to measure.

It is therefore essential to start small and aim to deliver quickly. An incremental approach can be taken and the grand schemes can evolve once confidence has been established in the basic tools being used.

7.3 BASIC MEASURES

Throughout the preceding text we have referred to the measurement of performance. In this section we shall look at what is meant by performance and suggest some basic measures for each dimension of performance.

7.3.1 The dimensions of performance

Performance can be viewed in three dimensions:

- Productivity: the cost (in effort) to produce a unit product
- Delivery: the elapsed time to produce a unit product
- Quality: either the degree to which the product satisfies the business need, or the extent to which the product delights the customer

Each of the dimensions of performance is expressed in terms of two components. They all have a component called product, and FPA provides a measure of product size. How FPA measures product size has been the subject of this book and the reader is referred back to Chapter 2 if in doubt.

Each dimension has one other component that is unique to that dimension. These are the cost, time and quality aspects, respectively. It is important that the components used are commonly defined and understood. If everyone is measuring the same things in the same way, then comparisons between projects, departments and even organizations may become more meaningful, although bear in mind the dangers outlined earlier in this chapter.

It is important to remember that to make full use of the information, for comparison etc., it is essential to know something about the environment in which the production took place. Measurements need to be taken of project environmental factors.

We shall examine each of the dimensions of performance in more depth shortly, but before that it is worth considering what exactly it is that we are measuring the performance of.

7.3.2 The process whose performance is to be measured

If asked to define the development process, different IS staff would offer different definitions. For instance, a programmer might say writing programs, a project manger might say developing new systems, a senior manager might say supplying the correct IT, and so on. None of the answers is wrong; they are all given from different perspectives. Understanding these perspectives and how they are to be helped by gathering metrics is a key factor in establishing a metrics programme. Basically, a process has to be defined and understood by all before it can be criticized, measured and improved.

Table 7.1 summarizes some of the perspectives that exist in a typical in-house IS department.

Table 7.1 Different managers' potential views of 'Production'

	Development	Support	Operations	Infrastructure
Senior manager	All	All	All	All
Project manager	All	Some	Some	Some
Support manager	Some	All	Some	Some
Technical manager	Some	Some	Some	All
Team leader	Some/none	Some/none	Some/none	Some/none

For the purposes of this chapter, we shall restrict ourselves to the development part of the production process. When the MKII technique was put into the public domain, the definition of the development part of the production process included all parts from the beginning of the analysis stage to the end of the implementation stage, i.e. all parts pre-analysis (e.g. feasibility studies) are excluded, as are all post-implementation parts (e.g. support).

Having defined the boundaries of the development process, the next step is to define the level at which performance is to be measured. For instance, if the metrics programme is to supply information on performance in the drawing of data flow diagrams, then the production process must be decomposed to a level where the drawing of data flow diagrams is distinguishable from other work. Figure 7.1 shows an example partial decomposition of the development process consistent with the boundaries defined above.

If a methodology is in place or internal standards have been produced then a development decomposition will be available. One could argue that if it is not available, then there is not a clearly defined and understood production process in the department. If this is the case it is unlikely that a metrics programme will help

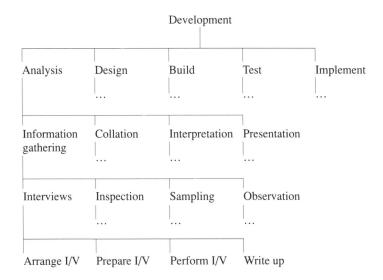

Figure 7.1 Development decomposed.

bring order to the chaos that probably exists, unless the department is very small and everybody has a shared mental model.

7.3.3 Productivity

Productivity can be expressed as product per unit of cost. The common alternative to our definition of productivity is to quote cost/unit of product. This has its merits, but most performance improvement programmes seek to increase performance. If the alternative definition of productivity was used, then cost reduction, i.e. productivity improvement, would actually result in a lower number. It is therefore usually less confusing to use the product per unit of cost definition, which increases as costs decrease.

Cost can be measured in two ways: money and effort. Normally effort can be expressed as money, although this is a complex procedure and is the province of management accountants. Most organizations using FPA use effort as their unit of cost. Various units of effort can be used, for instance:

- Work hour: an hour spent by one person working on production including minor breaks but excluding major breaks, such as lunch.
- Work day: a number of work hours; a day spent by one person working on production.
- Work week: a number of work hours; a number of work days; a week spent by one person working on production.
- Work month: a number of work hours; a number of work days; a number of work weeks; a month spent by one person working on production.

Whichever units of effort are decided upon it is important to define them clearly. There are, however, two things that should be borne in mind when choosing units. Firstly, the definition of work hour will be common (if the above definition was applied) across organizations. Work days and weeks will vary depending on how long the working day or week actually is in each organization. Thus using work hours will greatly simplify performance comparisons. Secondly, when deciding the units to be used it is worth remembering who will be supplying the information. Programmers and analysts tend to monitor their work by the hour and are often used to supplying time sheets showing hours worked. In the light of these considerations, work hours would seem the appropriate base unit for effort.

There is another aspect that needs to be defined in order to determine the total effort involved in producing the product. That is to determine who is to be included when effort is being totalled. When the MKII technique was placed in the public domain, these criteria were published as well. Simply, they are to include anyone working directly on the project according to the project requirements and for the project leader. This definition includes:

- The project team, i.e. analysts, designers etc.
- The project leader and any more senior staff employed on the project
- Specialist consultants brought in to provide specific services
- Users, where they are working on the project

but excludes:

- Users simply detailing their requirements or checking the deliverables
- Senior managers (except where working as above)
- Central support services, e.g. secretarial

7.3.4 Delivery

Delivery can be expressed as product per unit of elapsed time. Units of elapsed time are universal: seconds, minutes, hours, weeks, years etc. The unit of time that is commonly used to express delivery is weeks, resulting in function points per elapsed week.

Difficulties sometimes arise in organizations where there are delays between phases of projects. These delays can occur for many reasons: as an example consider the situation where the user department takes nine weeks to sign off the requirements and the development is thus halted for the nine weeks. The question is then should that delay be included when calculating delivery? The answer depends on what the purpose of measuring delivery is. If it is for projecting future delivery and the users will always take a long time, then it may be appropriate to include the time. If it is to see if a toolset improves delivery rate, then provide another metric which excludes it, called 'effective delivery'.

7.3.5 Quality

Quality is not as simple to define measures for as the other two dimensions. There are two main problems: the first relates to the definition of quality, and the second to the nature of measuring it.

For some reason, the definition of quality causes disputes between people working in the area. Generally though, all proffered definitions can be loosely summarized as one of the following:

- The fitness for purpose of the product, i.e. the fitness for the business purpose, not just whether it satisfies the specification (major disasters are often a result of incorrect specification).
- The extent to which the product delights the customers.

The first definition takes the view that there is an absolute where a product can be '100%'. For instance, if the only requirement for the product was to be able to use it to get once from London to Brighton, then a pedal cycle could be described as 100% fit for purpose and therefore of being 100% quality. This would be true even if the bicycle was rusty and bent, provided that it could make the journey required of it. It would clearly score fairly low under the second definition of quality, whereas a chauffeur-driven Rolls-Royce, say, would score much higher for most people.

These alternative definitions of quality pose a problem, since it is hard to generalize as to what quality is, much less to determine common measures for it. For the purposes of illustration in this section, we shall use the first definition of quality: that of fitness for purpose.

Having settled on a definition, we now require a way of expressing quality in terms of numbers. The most common method is to express quality in terms of defect density, sometimes thought of as the absence of quality since any defect is a quality failure. Thus we could have a measure: defects per unit of product.

Unlike the productivity and delivery measures which we would seek to maximize, the defect density is a measure that would be minimized, i.e. the measure becomes smaller.

There is one final consideration, however. That is, we have an opportunity to examine three different sorts of quality using our foregoing definition.

1. The quality of the product, i.e. do all the bits of the product, as supplied, operate correctly?
2. The quality of the process, i.e. how often did the product have to be reworked in order to achieve its quality as defined in point 1?
3. The functional quality of the product, i.e. does the product supply the functionality that the user wished for, but may not have expressed specifically, and is therefore delighted to find incorporated in the product. This is different from point 1. For instance, the chauffeur-driven Rolls-Royce could operate perfectly and score 0 defects under point 1, but fail to pass the requirement that it can be carried up a flight of stairs to be stored in the hallway of a flat.

Table 7.2 shows an example of part of a defect categorization that would allow analysis along the lines suggested above to be carried out.

Table 7.2 Defect categorization

Defect type	Cause	Impact
Off specification	Program flaw	System failure
Non-conformance	Design flaw	System interrupt
	Specification flaw	Inconvenience
		Immaterial

7.3.6 Project environmental factors

As mentioned above, methods used, people involved, tools and languages are examples of factors which affect the way a development project performs. It is necessary to identify which factors have an effect and how great an effect that is. Table 7.3 gives an example table that lists potential factors.

All of these factors will vary to some degree from organization to organization, and some from project to project. They can all alter the performance of IT production. For instance, a project being run by an experienced project manager using a recognized method will probably achieve higher productivity than one without those attributes (all other factors being equal).

At the end of a project, when its performance components are recorded, information about the type of project needs to be recorded as well. The type of project is defined with reference to the environmental factors which impacted it. Some of these factors are easily described in terms of numbers, while others such as user commitment cannot be measured and need to be classified or coded in some way.

Table 7.3 Project environmental factors

Machine characteristics, e.g.
  Type of machine
  Availability
Project attributes
  Methodology used
  Tools used
  Languages used
  Management methods
Personnel
  Management knowledge and experience
    of business area
    of technology
    of tools
    of methods
  Staff knowledge and experience
    of business area
    of technology
    of tools
    of methods
  User knowledge and experience
  Commitment
Environment
  Stability of requirement
  Surroundings
  Imposed constraints

For analysis purposes a common system of recording the factors is needed. Table 7.4 gives an example of how this might be done for the factors listed in Table 7.3.

The whole subject of capturing project environmental factors is less well defined than that of the performance dimensions, despite much work in the area. There are a number of project management books on the market, and various books that look at risk analysis. These, read in conjunction with books on metrics, will provide useful reference material for those interested in exploring the subject further.

7.3.7 How is all this to be recorded?

There are three aspects to consider when looking at how to record information generated by a metrics programme:

- How to capture periodic data, such as how staff expend effort.
- How to store irregular data, such as project estimates, end of project data etc.
- How to ensure the stored data is available for easy analysis and reporting.

Most departments have an existing time recording system: this may suffice, need modifications or replacement. If the system is to be replaced there are proprietary packages that perform some of the functions that have been discussed, though the system could be developed from scratch. Figure 7.2 gives an example of a list of requirements of a metrics repository and Fig. 7.3 gives an overview of the sort of metrics that would be required for such a system.

Table 7.4 Project environmental factor scoring sheet

1. Machine characteristics
   - (a) Type of machine   Make and Model:..

     PC.............. Mini ....M/F ....(Please tick)
   - (b) Availability   % Available
2. Project attributes
   - (a) Methodology used   Name..

     Approach   Trad .... 4GL......Prototype ....Package....................

     Other (specify) ....

     % tuning required.........
   - (b) Tools used (please name)   Analysis ....

     Build..

     Management ....
   - (c) Languages used   Name..
   - (d) Management methods   Name..

     % tuning required.........
3. Personnel
   - (a) Management knowledge and experience
     - of business area   Number of years.............
     - of technology   Number of years.............
     - of tools   Number of years.............
     - of methods   Number of years.............
   - (b) Staff knowledge and experience
     - of business area   Number of years.............
     - of technology   Number of years.............
     - of tools   Number of years.............
     - of methods   Number of years.............
   - (c) User knowledge and experience
     - of business area   Number of years.............
     - of technology   Number of years.............
     - of tools   Number of years.............
     - of methods   Number of years.............
     - Commitment   Score 1–3 ....1 = Antagonistic

       2 = Uninterested

       3 = Strongly in favour
4. Environment
   - Stability of requirement   Score 1–3 ....1 = Highly volatile

     2 = Changes

     3 = Static/fixed

     number of changes.........
   - Surroundings   Score 1–3 ....1 = Uncomfortable

     2 = Comfortable

     3 = Luxurious
   - Imposed constraints   Score 1–3 ....1 = Rigid imposed constraints

     2 = Rigid agreed constraints

     3 = No constraints

Levels of management affected
The system will need to provide information at a number of levels:

Project management
IT management
Organization management

Project management requirements
Project managers will need:

(a)   The ability to *interrogate* the system to obtain *relevant* past *performance figures* to help them in estimating their current project. They will need to know:

Expected effort: whole project and distributed by phase
Expected time-scales: whole project and distributed by phase
Expected quality of final system

Performance figures are ratios that give:

Productivity: product/effort
Delivery: product/time
Quality: product/defects

(b)   The ability to obtain *relevant work distribution models* for their current project. Work distribution models are models that show how effort and time have been expended on previous projects. They are an aid to high-level planning, costing and resourcing.
(c)   The ability to produce period end reports showing progress on the project against expectations, e.g. effort/cost/time discrepancies, problems encountered, expected problems.

IT management requirements
The managers of the IT function will want information to enable them to make comparisons between different areas of operation, e.g. methods, tools, techniques. They will also want departmental figures to help in estimating future staff requirements etc. They will need the following:

(a)   Reports summarizing *performance figures* by *project feature*.
(b)   The ability to interrogate the system on an *ad hoc* basis, e.g. to establish the frequency and impact of problem types or to establish the frequency and impact of unexpected work.

Organization management requirements
The organization will want periodic reports to help with assessing the efficiency of the IT department in providing solutions. They will want to compare the *cost of running IT* with the *product produced.*

(a)   Reports summarizing *performance figures* by *project feature*.
Project features are any features of a product that the management may want to investigate.
(b)   The ability to interrogate the system on an *ad hoc* basis, e.g. to establish the frequency and impact of problem types or to establish the frequency and impact of unexpected work.

Figure 7.2 Example Requirements of a metrics repository.

A key thing to remember is that different levels of staff take a different view of the organization. Most organizations will have roughly the following sorts of staff:

- Senior manager: views production as involving all of the areas of IT.
- Development project manager: concerned with those aspects that directly affect his or her project, i.e. all development and support, operations and infrastructure work when directly attributable.
- Support and infrastructure managers: concerned with performance in their areas.

Metrics required

Performance figures
To provide performance figures the following will be required:

Product size: measured in MK II function points
Effort: measured in work hours
Elapsed time: measured in elapsed weeks, from *start* to *end*
Defects: number of non-conformances at major project deliverable reviews

Work distribution models
To provide distribution models the following will be needed:

Standard phase definitions: from SSADM/PRINCE
Deviations from standard: planned and unplanned
Effort: for phase and deviation
Elapsed time: for phase and deviation

Period end reports
To provide these it will be necessary to hold:

Effort per period: planned and actual
Problems per period: categorized and quantified in terms of time/cost/effort
Tasks performed: standard and non-standard, expected and unexpected

Relevance
To enable the above to be relevant *project profile* will be necessary. This will consist of *project features* that will categorize the project.

Project profile: consists of project/environmental factors

Organization management reports
These require that projects can be costed and identified as delivered to the organization as a whole. There should also be a business benefit associated with each project.

Figure 7.3 Example metrics.

7.4 SUMMARY OF PERFORMANCE MEASUREMENT

There are two key points to make:

1. The requirements of the metrics programme will change with time. Make the programme and any system built to store the metrics as flexible as possible.
2. Do not attempt to measure too much in the early days. People will regard the supply of information as an imposition if there is too much involved. Additionally, until you have collected some information you do not know what else you need to know.

7.5 PROJECT ESTIMATING

The size of the product is a major driver in calculating project costs and time-scales. In IT projects the product, i.e. the system, is measured in function points. By estimating the function point index (FPI) the following can in turn be estimated:

- Effort
- Duration
- Headcount

The remainder of this chapter describes the steps involved in the estimating process. A worked example from the Elbert Super Car system is provided by way of illustration.

7.5.1 Overview of estimating

There are two major categories of estimating method: those which are top-down and those which are bottom-up. Some tools and techniques combine each approach.

Whichever estimating approach you use, always use another in order to check that the main one is reasonable. If you only look at one watch you have no idea whether it is correct. If you confirm it against another timepiece then you can greatly increase your confidence in the time you have read off the watch. The same holds true for estimating.

7.5.2 Top-down

Top-down techniques generate estimates based on the functional and technical requirements of the system. The MKII FPA technique is an *algorithmic* top-down technique. Each technique has its own approach, but the principle is still the same, i.e. the detailed tasks required to complete the project are unknown and therefore knowledge of the development process performance is required in order to generate an estimate based on the requirements of the system.

The simplest top-down approach is known as *estimating by analogy*. The principle is that the proposed project is compared with previous projects that have completed. The estimator will look for projects built in a similar environment by staff with similar skills, and will try to find projects that 'feel' as if they were of a similar 'size'. 'Size' in this context does not refer to the FPI, but to the estimator's gut-feel for the project. In this form it is more accurate than taking a guess, but less accurate than formal methods such as FPA.

Tools that are based on the analogy approach improve their estimates by providing detailed classification and categorization of key project parameters. This reduces the reliance on the estimator's gut-feel for the project.

Algorithmic techniques, such as FPA, have defined formulae that are applied to quantified project characteristics. These are used to generate the project estimate. In the case of FPA, the formulae should be calibrated to suit the environment in which the estimate is being produced, although less reliable results are obtainable using industry average calibrations.

Top-down estimating is generally more accurate at the early stages of the life cycle, but toward the latter parts of the design phase bottom-up estimating will become more accurate.

7.5.3 Bottom-up estimating

Bottom-up techniques rely on breaking the project down into a series of known tasks of a short duration, estimating each task individually, and then summing the tasks to give a total project estimate.

In the early phases of the project, bottom-up techniques can be reasonably successfully applied to generate estimates and schedules for the next phase. They are not normally reliable for generating total project estimates until you get to the latter part of the design phases. One of the reasons for this is that until you know how many program modules you are to write, it's hard to estimate how long they will take to do.

7.5.4 The steps involved in estimating

There are seven steps to producing an FPA estimate:

1. Identify and size the logical transactions
2. Using performance data calculate the normative project effort and duration
3. Allocate effort and duration to the phases of the project
4. Adjust the effort and duration to account for project environmental factors
5. Consider project deadlines and adjust the effort and schedule accordingly
6. Calculate headcount by project phase
7. Revise headcounts by phase in line with known staffing constraints, recalculate the effort and duration

In order to explain the steps, we will carry on with the worked example from Chapter 3 where we estimated the size of the Elbert Super Car's front desk system. At the end of this chapter there is a case study example for the reader to try, with a worked answer in Appendix F.

Step 1: Identify and size the logical transactions

The first step in the estimating process is to establish the size of the product for which you wish to estimate the development cost. The approach to this will depend on the current project stage:

- Pre-logical design (refer to Chapter 3)
- Post-logical design (refer to Chapter 4)
- Enhancements (refer to Chapter 6)

Many projects end up as a mix of new development and enhancement. It is usual to find different productivity levels for the different categories of work. In order to account for this in the estimate it is necessary to size the two types of work separately. Thus, while identifying logical transactions and sizing the work to be done in each, note against them whether they are new or enhanced.

FPA can be used for sizing individual changes and the changes can then be estimated in the same way as for new development. There is a potential danger in that the smaller the enhancement, the less influence the size of the change has on driving the cost of implementing it. This must be borne in mind when using the technique for projects less than about 30 function points in size. With projects this small, there can be an appreciable non-size-dependent cost due to factors such as:

- time to familiarize staff with the work
- time to set up the project
- time to document the work

Step 2: Calculate the normative project effort and duration

The effort and duration are calculated with reference to measures of IS performance. For instance, if we know that we produce 0.1 function points per work hour on an average project of this type and size, then we can calculate the effort required to complete our project. This is known as a *normative* estimate, since it is an estimate for an average project, having been generated from an analysis of previous projects.

In order to select the correct productivity and delivery figures to use, it is necessary to classify the project so that figures for previous similar projects can be identified. The classification should be made on the basis of the project environmental factors. The project estimator must assess the degree to which each of the relevant factors is present in the project under examination to select the appropriate source data for estimating purposes. An approach taken in most organizations is to regularly publish the productivity–size and delivery–size relationships, together with other calibratable factors (see later steps) for each of the environments for which data is available. This greatly reduces the amount of research the estimator must do.

In practice, metrics databases do not contain sufficient projects to produce statistically reliable average productivity and delivery figures for all the potential project environments. While this is less than ideal, a pragmatic approach that has been tested in a number of organizations will still produce good estimates.

The basis is to minimize the number of environments considered. For instance, a good starting point is to differentiate only between on-line and batch work, and between new development and enhancement. Having done this, calculate the FPI for each environment and for the total system, i.e. sum the FPI for on-line new development, for batch new development and so on. You will now have up to four subtotals and an overall size.

The next step is to chose the appropriate productivity figure. Charles Symons (1991, pp. 141–4) showed a link between project size and productivity, and between project size and delivery. This has been reconfirmed by members of the UK Function Point User Group. The relationship between size and productivity is such that as size increases, up to a size of around 300 function points, productivity rises. After this size, productivity starts to fall and levels off at about 1000 function points. The exact points at which the rise, fall and levelling occur vary from organization to organization. Figure 7.4 is a graph showing the industry average productivity–size relationship. Theories have been offered to explain the relationship. The simplest is that small projects tend to have large fixed overheads, and that larger projects have increasing management and team communication problems. These problems probably limit at a certain impact, hence the levelling off of the productivity value i.e. productivity does not drop to zero.

Thus, for each environment obtain a productivity figure based on the total project size (since it is the total project size that affects productivity). Then for each environment calculate the effort as follows:

$$effort = size/productivity$$

Finally, sum the effort figures for each environment to give the total project effort.

A situation faced by all organizations that wish to start using FPA is that they do not have their own calibrated figures for the productivity–size relationship until they have been using FPA for some time. This can be frustrating, because there is often a desire to start gaining the benefits associated with using a formal estimating technique. In these circumstances it is possible to make cautious use of the industry averages published for productivity and reproduced in Fig. 7.4. These offer only two different environments, those of 3GLs and 4GLs. Figure 7.4 shows Charles Symons' industry average productivity figures for a 3GL environment expressed in function points per work hour. Symons indicates that multiplying the figures for 3GL by 1.5 gives rough figures for a 4GL environment.

For the purposes of the worked example we shall assume that the system is to be entirely built using a 3GL. The FPI was calculated in Chapter 3 as 325. With reference to Fig. 7.4, the effort will be:

$$effort = 325/0.12 = 2708 \text{ hours}$$

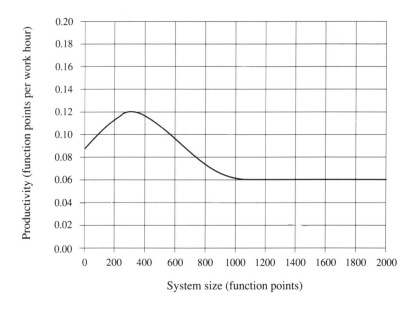

Figure 7.4 Industry average productivity–size relationship (from Symons, 1991, p. 141).

Finally we must calculate the duration. This is done by using the appropriate delivery figure. Again this varies with size, and Charles Symons found the relationship to be such that delivery varies with square root of size. The effect of this is that delivery increases with project size, but as project size becomes larger the rate of increase of delivery slows down. This becomes more understandable when you consider two factors. First, large teams are needed to deal with large projects, and large teams are less productive than small teams due to a variety of factors, including the complexity of managing them and the inter-team communication difficulties. Secondly, organizations have finite resources and therefore a practical limit to the amount of work they can accomplish in a given time. As this limit is reached the effect of inefficiencies becomes more marked and reduces the amount of extra work that can be done for an increase in effort.

Symons offers an industry average figure which can be used in the absence of in-house measurement:

$$\text{Delivery} = 0.45 \times \text{square root of size}$$

For our 325 function point system this gives us a delivery rate of:

$$\text{Delivery} = 0.45 \times \text{root}(325) = 8.11 \text{ function points per elapsed week}$$

From this the duration can be calculated as:

$$\text{Duration} = \text{Size}/\text{Delivery}$$
$$= 325/8.11 = 40 \text{ weeks}$$

While the industry average figures provide a useful starting point, performance varies greatly from one organization to the next. If you do use them as a starting point, attempt to collect your own data as soon as possible in order to produce calibrated figures. Even data on a few projects that you are sure are reasonably typical will allow you to start modifying the industry average figures to reflect your organization.

Step 3: Allocate effort and duration to the phases of the project

At this point we have a figure for the total effort and duration of an average project to build the system that we sized in step 1. Step 3 allocates the effort and duration to the project phases.

Table 7.5 shows the industry standard model quoted by Charles Symons (1991, p. 157).

The effort and elapsed time are distributed over a project lifecycle in accordance with the relevant percentages. It is essential that an appropriate model for the type of project being undertaken is selected. Where appropriate models are not available, the industry average model can be used. It is normal, however, for organizations to produce their own calibrated models for each major development approach.

For our example we will use the industry average model. The project effort was 2708 hours and the elapsed time was 40 weeks, see Table 7.6.

Table 7.5 Industry standard model for allocating effort and elapsed time to each project phase

Phase	% Effort	% Elapsed time
Analysis	22	35
Design	15	15
Code	46	25
Test	12	15
Install	5	10

Table 7.6 Total effort and elapsed time

Phase	Effort (hours)	Elapsed time (weeks)
Analysis	596	14
Design	406	6
Code	1246	10
Test	325	6
Install	135	4

Step 4: Adjust the effort and duration to account for project environmental factors

We now have an estimate, by phase, showing the effort and duration for an *average* project. What we almost certainly do not have, though, is an average project; rather, one that will deviate in some way from a straight arithmetical average of all projects. We must now make adjustments to account for these deviations and thus consideration is given to the environmental factors. For instance, if all previous projects were carried out using a standard development life cycle and this project is to use prototyping, an assessment must be made as to how this affects the productivity, delivery and work distribution.

Some account has been taken of environmental factors when the productivity and delivery figures were selected. If the project environment matches that of the projects from which the calibration was derived, then there should be no problem. Careful sifting through data for previous projects will help, but estimators also have to rely on their own experience and judgement. The fact that we are considering each phase separately helps, since it provides a structured way of thinking about the total project. For example, we may know that a new diagramming tool will be used to model the requirements, that the analyst is extremely experienced, and that the users are knowledgeable about their requirements. Under these circumstances we would probably wish to reduce both the elapsed weeks and effort figures for the analysis phase. The amount of reduction will have to be estimated based on our own knowledge of the situation. We could then move on to consider the design phase.

Having adjusted the effort and duration by phase as necessary, a new value for total project effort and total duration should be calculated.

Whatever adjustments are made (or indeed not made), it is vital to log the reasons so that an end of project review can understand how the estimate was derived. This will then allow the estimating process to be improved when the next calibration is produced.

For our case study we shall assume that there is insufficient environment information to make any changes.

Step 5: Consider project deadlines and adjust the effort and schedule accordingly

If a deadline is imposed for project completion, then this clearly affects the length of time the project can take. If the available time is less than the estimated elapsed time then a schedule compression factor (SCF) can be calculated:

$$SCF = \text{available time/estimated elapsed time}$$

This figure is a good indicator of the risk involved in the imposed deadline. As the SCF falls below 0.85, the risk of the project failing to be completed increases.

The SCF is used to revise the effort for each phase as follows:

$$\text{New effort} = \text{old effort/SCF}$$

The elapsed time simply becomes the available time.

The effect of the effort adjustment is to raise the total effort required for a project when the project is forced to respect a deadline that was less than the estimated duration. This effect has been noted by a number of researchers and the authors suggest that the reader consult one of the many project management handbooks that are available. Briefly, the reasons are generally held to be that shortened duration requires more team members. This leads to increased communication within the team and increased management overhead.

In our example, we shall assume that there is a 38 week deadline on the project. This yields an SCF of:

$$38/40 = 0.95$$

This is then used to recalculate the phase effort using the above formula. The elapsed time for each phase is recalculated on the basis of a total of 38 weeks available. The result is shown in Table 7.7.

Table 7.7 Recalculating effort and elapsed time

Phase	Effort	Elapsed time
Analysis	627	13
Design	427	6
Code	1312	9
Test	342	6
Install	142	4

This gives a revised total project estimate of 2850 hours over 38 weeks.

Step 6: Calculate headcount by project phase

Given the effort for a phase and its duration, it is possible to calculate the headcount required. Again, Charles Symons (1991, p. 161) offers industry standard numbers, but these should be adjusted for your organization.

The headcount per phase can be calculated as:

$$Headcount = constant \times work\ hours/elapsed\ weeks$$

The constant is calculated from the number of working hours in a week and the assumed staff utilization. This will vary from organization to organization. Remember to allow for holidays, training and sickness levels. The industry standard constant is based on 65% utilization over a 35 hour week:

$$1/(0.65 \times 35) = 0.044$$

In our example, we shall use 0.044 as the constant in the above formula and calculate the headcount as in Table 7.8.

Table 7.8 Calculating headcount

Phase	Headcount	Effort	Elapsed time
Analysis	2.12	627	13
Design	3.13	427	6
Code	6.4	1312	9
Test	2.5	342	6
Install	1.56	142	4

Step 7: Revise headcounts in line with known staffing constraints

Having calculated the ideal staffing levels, it is necessary to adjust them to match known staffing constraints, and also to round them, since, for example, 6.4 programmers are hard to find.

The effect of rounding and adjusting will be two-fold. First, the duration for the affected phase will change, since the number of people involved has changed; for instance, rounding 6.4 down to 6 will cause the duration to increase. The second effect was described in step 5, that is a change in headcount will cause a change in effort due to management overhead, team communication etc.

A point to consider here is that if there are deadlines there is no point in rounding down all the headcounts such that the deadline is missed.

When adjusting headcount, a two step process is followed for *each* phase. The first step is to calculate a rounding adjustment factor (RAF) for the phase:

$$RAF = root(rounded\ headcount) / root(unrounded\ headcount)$$

where root is the square root.

Having calculated the RAF for the phase, the effort and duration are adjusted as follows:

New effort   = old effort × RAF
New elapsed = old elapsed/RAF

For our worked example we shall round up to the nearest half person or whole person, as in Table 7.9. This gives us a final total project estimate of 2958 hours over 36 weeks. If we are monitoring IS performance, then it is useful to calculate the estimated productivity and delivery of the project. In the case of our worked example these are:

$$Productivity = 325/2958 = 0.11$$
$$Delivery\ \ \ \ = 325/36 = 9.03$$

These compare with the normative productivity and delivery of 0.12 and 8.11 respectively, which we used to calculate the effort and duration originally. In other words we have traded productivity for delivery and are estimating that this project will complete faster than an average project, but will be less productive.

Table 7.9 Final project estimate

Phase	Headcount	Effort	Elapsed time
Analysis	2.5	681	12
Design	3.5	452	5.7
Code	6.5	1322	8.9
Test	2.5	342	6
Install	2	161	3.5

7.5.5 Estimating wisdom

The above technique appears to be very precise since it generates numbers to decimal point accuracy. As with all estimating, remember that this is only an estimate. When the end of the estimating process is reached, round the numbers appropriately. If people see numbers precise to a decimal place, or even to the nearest 10 hours they will often assume that the figures are accurate. With the above example it may be worth quoting the effort estimate as 3000 hours, or even round all the phases up to the nearest 50 or 100 and then recalculate the total estimate. Similarly, the duration figures will need to be rounded.

When estimating there is no crystal ball. No technique in existence will give you the right answer until the project is completed and the effort and duration are known. That said, the FPA technique is capable of calibration, and thus can be improved as data from completed projects is gathered.

7.5.6 Calibration

All of the constants in each of the above steps can be calibrated. The process of calibration is not for the faint-hearted though, and requires a statistical background and a good spreadsheet.

Detailed explanation would take a book in itself. The following is an outline of the approach adopted by the authors.

Step 1: Collect project data

The amount of data required will depend upon the variability of projects in your organization. A reasonable start can be made with as few as 10 projects, but these would all have to be from a similar environment. That said, if we assume that we have the following four environments initially:

- New development, on-line
- New development, batch
- Enhancement, on-line
- Enhancement, batch

then we would only require 40 projects to have 10 in each environment. A quick survey of projects completed in the last year would probably provide sufficient data for many organizations. The data we require by environment is at minimum:

- UFP by environment: to gather this, mark each logical transaction with its predominant environment. Some will fall out with the classification, for instance an on-line screen kicking off a batch report. These could be marked as belonging to another environment, and then if there are insufficient of them when producing the calibration to justify attempting to deal with them separately, include them with one of the other environments
- Effort spent on the UFP in that environment: unfortunately, projects do not typically record how much time was spent designing new batch transactions, analysing on-line enhancements etc. Thus we must make educated guesses based on the time recording that we have. To do this, log the total project time and then ask the project leader to judge the percentage time spent on new development versus enhancement. Then ask them to judge, for the new development, the percentage on-line versus batch. Repeat for enhancements. (Note: extending this to asking them to judge relative percentage effort spent on inputs, processing and outputs for each environment would allow the weights W_i, W_e and W_o to be calibrated. In practice, this does not appear to be worthwhile in most organizations.)
- Environmental factors: in the absence of a formal method of logging this information, simply ask the project leader to identify factors that affected the project. Prompt if necessary with a list of typical factors, but do not limit responses to within the list.
- Headcount, effort and duration by phase: effort and duration should be readily available, and should be recorded in the units used on site (see earlier section on performance measurement). Headcount should be the average full-time equivalent headcount and may require some judgement by the project leader.

Step 2: Identify useful environment categories

This may seem like an odd second step, since step 1 required us to classify transactions by environment, but until we have collected data about the factors that impact projects it is difficult to establish definitive environment categories for any given calibration. For the first few calibrations, unless you have a tremendous amount of data available, it is probably wise to stay with the initial categories that you have identified.

Having selected the environment categories, for each plot productivity versus size and delivery versus size.

Step 3: Draw smoothed productivity size and delivery size curves

By this stage in the process, some form of computer tool will be essential. A spreadsheet fulfils the requirements quite adequately. Some spreadsheets will plot the lines for you, or you may prefer to draw them by eye.

Step 4: Spot outliers

By this stage, you will have a number of graphs (eight if you have followed the suggested environments), each with a set of data points and either a productivity–size curve or a delivery–size curve superimposed. In an ideal world the points would all lie neatly along the line. It is more likely that the points will be fairly well scattered. This step is designed to try and account for some of the more extreme variation.

The approach is to identify the projects that quite simply do not appear to fit in with the rest. These are the ones that are furthest from the line, the ones out on their own. Having done so, read through the project data, if necessary contacting the project leaders, to identify reasons for the differences. Those for which the difference can be explained (for instance 'We completed slower than normal because the team leader was changed four times and the programmers were all graduate trainees') should be removed from the general pool of projects being considered. At the end of the calibration process though, revisit them and see if it possible to produce general guidance, e.g. 'When faced with probable staff changes and graduate trainees, add $x\%$ to the project effort and $y\%$ to duration'.

Step 5: Redraw the smoothed curves

Having removed the outliers, it may be necessary to redraw the curves. Consider repeating step 4, but be wary of excluding all your data. Removing too many outliers is simply another way of attempting to define other environments. If there are a low number of projects, then this would be undesirable.

Step 6: Using the smoothed curves estimate the projects

Working with the list of logical transactions and the productivity–size and duration–size graphs, produce normative estimates for the projects that were left after the outliers were removed. Do not attempt to make any adjustments for other environmental factors, but do apply headcount rounding.

In order to apply headcount rounding, it will be necessary to take the normative estimates and spread the effort and duration across the phases of the projects. The correct percentages to apply in order to spread effort and duration across each phase can be worked out by taking the average for all the projects that you are working with. Finally, calculate what the headcount should have been and then apply the rounding formulae based on what the headcount actually was.

Having produced the estimates including headcount rounding, plot the resultant predicted project effort against the actual project effort and investigate those projects which are outliers. Those whose variance is explicable should be removed, but bear in mind steps 4 and 5 above.

Step 7: Vary the headcount adjustment formula to try to improve the fit

The headcount adjustment formula was quoted as:

$$\text{RAF} = \text{root(rounded headcount)}/\text{root(unrounded headcount)}$$

When the formula was presented, the root was stated to be the square root. This can of course be varied and different roots can be tried to see if the fit improves. There is also an implied constant term in the above. The RAF could always be multiplied by a set amount, or always have a set amount added to, or subtracted from it. Try different values and see what effect this has on the fit.

It is very easy to get carried away and over analyse the situation. Bear in mind the 80:20 rule: 80% of the results are normally achieved at a cost of 20% of the effort.

Step 8: Adjust the productivity–size and delivery–size relationships to try and improve the fit

This step and step 7 should be iterated as often as necessary in order to 'fine tune' the estimate.

If the data have been set up on a spreadsheet it should be a simple matter to alter the productivity–size and delivery–size relationships and then allow the spreadsheet to do the work.

As with any activity such as this, keep an eye on the numbers that you are producing. It is all too easy to produce a set of figures that explain the projects you have, but which are seriously distorted by one or two projects which were subject to odd environmental factors. A useful figure to keep an eye on is the percentage error, i.e. the difference between the estimated effort and the actual effort. It is usually possible to reduce this drastically during the first pass through steps 7 and 8, and then find only marginal improvements on future passes. This can be a guide as to when to stop iterating through these steps.

Step 9: Use the resultant calibrations to estimate completed projects that were not among the original pool

As a final check, repeat step 6 but for projects which were not included during the calibration process. It may be necessary to reserve a random sample before beginning step 1, or if you are in a situation where projects are completing while you are doing the calibration you may be able to use these projects.

The results you get with these projects will give you an idea of how good (or bad) the calibration is. If data are available on the accuracy of other estimating techniques in your organization, then the calibration can be compared with those. Remember that you must compare like with like. FPA is a top-down technique particularly suited to estimating early in the life-cycle. There is no point in comparing its accuracy with, say, an estimate derived from the actuals for the analysis and design phases, combined with a bottom-up estimate for the build phase.

Calibration conclusion

The above can be a long process, and can take many iterations before a useful result is obtained. The results, though, are much improved estimates. Successive calibrations become more accurate. At UK Function Point User Group meetings, various organizations have verified the effectiveness of the process.

7.6 CONCLUSION

This chapter has laid out some ways in which FPA and associated metrics can be used. Whether or not it brings benefit to an organization depends not on the measurements taken but the skill with which they are interpreted.

For instance, if a building costs 10 times the amount estimated it is unlikely to be the fault of the estimating guidebook. It is more likely to be a poor assessment of the problem: inadequate specification of requirements, materials, risks etc. The person who would be to blame would be the architect/surveyor who was managing the project, not the bricklayer or carpenter. IT is just beginning to accept the fact that an estimating guidebook is possible. In future such a guide will be seen as essential, but its use will involve training.

The acceptance of the concept of measuring IT products and processes and recording the figures is an important step toward establishing a true discipline of software engineering.

7.7 KEY POINTS

- Any metrics programme should start small, aim to give rapid results, and be targeted in the areas of greatest need. It, and any systems supporting it, must be flexible enough to cope with the inevitable changes in the requirements of the metrics programme.
- Performance must be measured in all three dimensions of productivity, delivery and quality.
- Project environmental factors must be recorded and used in the analysis of performance variation.
- Reliance should never be placed on a single estimate; always produce at minimum two estimates using different techniques, and, if possible, different people.

- The FPA estimating technique should be calibrated both for the organization, and to account for the different project environments within the organization

7.8 CASE STUDY

Estimate the effort, duration and headcount for the practice administration system that was the subject of the case study in Chapter 3. The following assumptions should be made:

- TCA is 0.85
- The project will all be written in a 3GL
- The industry average productivity and delivery relationships apply
- The analysis effort will increase by 50 hours because of poor documentation of an existing small system
- The deadline for delivery is 35 weeks

Unadjusted function point totals can be found in Appendix B, which is the sample answer for the Chapter 3 case study. A sample solution for this case study exercise can be found in Appendix F.

APPENDIX A: TECHNICAL COMPLEXITY ADJUSTMENT

1. Data communications

For terminals connected remotely or locally; score as:

0   Batch processing or standalone PC
1   Batch with remote data entry or printing
2   Batch with remote data entry *and* printing
3   On-line data collection front end
4   More than front end but only 1 TP comms protocol
5   More than front end, more than 1 TP comms protocol

2. Distributed data processing

Distributed data or processing incorporated in applications; score as:

0   Application does not aid transfer of data or processing between components of system
1   Application prepares data for end-user processing on PC
2   Application prepares data for processing on different machine (not end-user)
3   Distributed processing, on-line, data transfer in one direction only
4   Distributed processing, on-line, data transfer in both directions
5   Processing dynamically performed on most appropriate component of system

3. Performance

Application performance objectives, agreed by the user, influence the design, development, installation and support (consider response times etc.); score as:

0   No requirement
1   Performance requirements stated and reviewed but no action
2   On-line response critical during peak hours. No special design for CPU utilization. Processing deadline is next business day

3   On-line response critical during business day. No special design for CPU utilization. Processing deadline affected by interfacing systems
4   Performance requirements need performance analysis during design
5   Performance analysis tools used in design, development and installation

4. Heavily used configuration

Target configuration heavily used and need is taken into account in development (consider effect of development/enhancement on the rest of the systems); score as:

0   Dedicated target configuration
1   Target configuration used but no effect on development
2   Target configuration has service level requirements
3   Part of the application needs tailoring to fit an existing configuration
4   There are operational restrictions that affect the whole application on a single processor
5   In addition the machine has distributed processors that have operational restrictions

5. Transaction rates

The transaction rate influences design, development, installation and support of the system (consider ability to cope with high rate of usage); score as:

0   No peak anticipated
1   10% of transactions affected by peak traffic
2   50% of transactions affected by peak traffic
3   All transactions affected by peak traffic
4   Performance analysis tasks in design phase
5   Performance analysis tools used in design, development and installation

6. On-line data entry

Score as:

0   All transactions batch
1   1%–7% interactive
2   8%–15% interactive
3   16%–23% interactive
4   24%–30% interactive
5   > 30% interactive

7. End-user efficiency

Users require on-line functions to help in the use of the system, e.g.:

• Navigational aids
• Menus
• On-line help

- Automated cursor movement
- Scrolling
- Remote printing
- Function keys
- Batch jobs from on-line transactions
- Cursor selection of screen data
- Heavy use of monitor facilities (colour, highlighting etc.)
- Hard copy of on-line transactions
- Mouse
- Windows
- Minimum screens
- Bilingual
- Multilingual

Score as:

0   None of the above
1   1–3 of the above
2   4–5 of the above
3   > 6 of the above
4   Plus design tasks for human factors
5   Special tools needed to demonstrate human factors objectives have been met

8. On-line update

Data is updated in *real time*, i.e. the system reflects the real world; score as:

0   None
1   On-line update is provided by system software
2   On-line update is provided by system software, but special design and build procedures need to be followed
3   As 2 but recovery routines needed
4   Transaction logging procedures needed
5   Transaction processing monitoring needed

9. Complex processing

Internal complexity beyond that dealt with by the entity counting conventions of MKII FPA.
  Which of the following characteristics apply to the application?

- Sensitive control (for example, special audit processing) and/or application specific security processing
- Extensive logical processing
- Extensive mathematical processing
- Much exception processing, many incomplete transactions, and much reprocessing of transactions
- Complex processing to handle multiple I/O possibilities; for example, multimedia, device independence

Score as:

0   None of the above applies
1   1 of the above
2   2 of the above
3   3 of the above
4   4 of the above
5   All of the above apply

10. Usable in other applications

The code is designed to be shared with or used by other applications. Do not confuse with factor 13.
   Score as:

0   No reusable code
1   Reusable code is used within the application
2   < 10% of the system considered for reuse
3   ≥ 10% of the system considered for reuse
4   Application was specifically packaged/documented to aid reuse, and application customized at source code level
5   Application was specifically packaged/documented to aid reuse, and was customized by means of parameters

11. Installation ease

Score as:

0   No special conversion and installation considerations were stated by the user
1   No special conversion and installation considerations were stated by the user *but* special setup required for installation
2   Conversion and installation requirements were stated by the user and conversion and installation guides were provided and tested
3   Conversion and installation requirements were stated by the user and conversion and installation guides were provided and tested. The impact was considered important
4   In addition to 2, conversion and installation tools were provided and tested
5   In addition to 3, conversion and installation tools were provided and tested

12. Operations ease

Score as:

0   No special operation considerations were stated by the user
1–4 Select from the following, each has a point value of 1 unless otherwise indicated:

- Application-specific start up, backup and recovery processes were required, provided and tested but operator intervention necessary
- Application-specific start up, backup and recovery processes were required, provided and tested and no operator intervention necessary (2 points)

- The application minimizes the need for tape mounts
- The application minimizes the need for paper handling

5 Application is designed for unattended operation. This means *no operator intervention* other than startup and shutdown. Error recovery is automatic

13. Multiple sites

Score as:

0 No user requirement to consider the needs of more than one user site
1 Multiple sites considered in design, but there would be identical hardware and software
2 Multiple sites considered in design, but there would be similar hardware and software
3 Multiple sites considered in design, but there would be different hardware and software

Add 1 for each of the following:

- Documentation and support plan are provided and tested to support the application at multiple sites
- The sites are in different countries

14. Facilitate change

The application has been specifically designed and developed to facilitate future change to user requirements.
Add scores for each of the following factors:

0 No special user requirement to design the application to minimize or facilitate change
1 Flexible query capability is provided that can handle simple logical enquiries
2 Flexible query capability is provided that can handle average logical enquiries
3 Flexible query capability is provided that can handle complex logical enquiries

Add for the following:

1 Significant control data is kept in tables that are maintained with on-line interactive processes with changes taking effect on next business day
2 Significant control data is kept in tables that are maintained with on-line interactive update

15. Requirements of other applications

Score as:

0 The system is completely standalone
1–4 System requirements for interfaces or data sharing have to be synchronized with other applications. Count 1 for each application up to 4
5 System requirements have to be synchronized with several (>4) other applications

16. Security, privacy, auditability

Add scores as follows:

1   If a system has to meet personal (maybe legal) privacy requirements
1   If the system has to meet special auditability requirements
2   If the system has to meet exceptional security requirements to prevent loss, e.g. of a financial nature
1   If encryption of data communications is required

17. User training needs

Score as:

0   If no special user training material or courses are developed
1   Standard tutorial help provided
2   Hypertext style tutorial help provided
3   Training course material provided
4   On-line training course material provided
5   Requirements for a separate complete system or simulator for training purposes

18. Direct use by third parties

Score as:

0   No third party connection to the system
1   Data is sent to or received from known third parties
2   Known third parties (closed user group) are connected directly to the system in read-only mode
3   Known third parties are connected directly to the system with on-line update capability
4   Known third parties are connected directly to the system with on-line create and delete capability
5   Unknown third parties (e.g. the general public, or a group too large to receive individual training or support) can access the system

19. Documentation

Count 1 for each documentation type listed below that is delivered and is up-to-date at the end of the project:

- User requirements definition
- User design (logical design/functional design)
- Technical design
- Program documentation (at least flow charts)
- Data element library
- Data element/record/program cross-reference
- Operations manual
- User manual

- System overview or brochure
- Test data library
- System cost–benefit tracking documents
- Change request/error report log

Score as:

0	If 0–2 documentation types
1	If 3–4 documentation types
2	If 5–6 documentation types
3	If 7–8 documentation types
4	If 9–10 documentation types
5	If 11–12 documentation types

APPENDIX B: SAMPLE SOLUTION FOR CHAPTER 3 CASE STUDY

B.1 LIST OF CLASSIFIED TRANSACTIONS

Transactions	CRUD	Complexity
Patient transactions		
Produce letters	E	A
Produce reprimands	E	A
Reception transactions		
Appointments booking		
Enquire	E	A
Make appointments	C	A
Change appointments	U	A
Cancel appointments	D	
Emergency appointments	C	A
Home visits		
Enquire	E	A
Book visits	C	A
Change visits	U	A
Cancel visits	D	
Emergency visits	C	A
Produce details for reception	E	C
Doctor transactions		
Produce surgery lists for doctor	E	C
Produce home visit lists for doctor	E	C
Doctor changes to surgery appointments	U	A
Doctor changes to home visit appointment	U	A
Administration transactions		
Patient registration		
Enquire	E	A
Add a patient	C	A
Alter patient details	U	A
Delete a patient	D	
Clinic format administration		
Enquire	E	C
Add a clinic format type	C	C
Change a clinic format type	U	C
Delete a clinic format type	D	

Transactions	CRUD	Complexity
Surgery format administration		
Enquire	E	C
Add a surgery format type	C	C
Change a surgery format type	U	C
Delete a surgery format type	D	
Timetables		
Create daily clinic timetables	C	C
Create daily surgery timetables	C	C
Change daily clinic timetables	U	C
Change daily surgery timetables	U	C

B.2 UFP MATRIX

	Simple	Average	Complex
Create/update	0×4 UFPs	10×12 UFPs	8×20 UFPs
Enquire/report	0×3 UFPs	5×10 UFPs	5×17 UFPs
Delete		5×8 UFPs	

Total unadjusted function point count = 455

B.3 ASSESSING THE SIZE OF EACH TRANSACTION

Transactions	Input	Entities	Output
Patient transactions			
Produce letters	1	5	7
Produce reprimands	1	10	7
Reception transactions			
Appointments booking			
Enquire	3	6	8
Make appointments	8	6	1
Change appointments	8	6	1
Cancel appointments	3	6	1
Emergency appointments	10	6	1
Home visits			
Enquire	3	6	10
Book visits	10	6	1
Change visits	10	6	1
Cancel visits	3	6	1
Emergency visits	10	6	1
Reports			
Produce details for reception	1	7	15
Doctor transactions			
Produce surgery lists for Doctor	1	7	10
Produce home visit lists for Doctor	1	7	12
Doctor changes to surgery appointments	8	6	1
Doctor changes to home visit appointment	8	6	1

Transactions	Input	Entities	Output
Administration transactions			
Patient registration			
Enquire	2	2	24
Add a patient	24	2	1
Alter patient details	24	2	1
Delete a patient	2	2	1
Clinic format administration			
Enquire	1	1	15
Add a clinic format type	15	1	1
Change a clinic format type	15	1	1
Delete a clinic format type	1	2	1
Surgery format administration			
Enquire	1	1	15
Add a surgery format type	15	1	1
Change a surgery format type	15	1	1
Delete a surgery format type	1	2	1
Timetables			
Create daily clinic timetables	5	3	1
Create daily surgery timetables	5	3	1
Change daily clinic timetables	5	3	1
Change daily surgery timetables	5	3	1
Totals	*225*	*138*	*146*

$$\text{UFP} = 0.58 \times 225 + 1.66 \times 138 + 0.26 \times 146 = 398$$

B.4 THE DATA APPROACH

Entity sizes were estimated as:

Entity	Attributes
Appointment slot	4
Clinic event	17
Clinic format	15
Doctor	4
Emergency appointment	4
Emergency home visit	10
Home visit	10
Home visit list	10
Patient	20
Patient type	4
Surgery event	17
Surgery format	15

Number of attributes (N_a) = 130
Number of entities (N_e) = 12
Number of relations (N_r) = 15

$$
\begin{aligned}
\text{Number of input fields} &= \{2N_a[1 + (N_r/N_e)]\} + 2N_e \\
&= \{2 \times 130 \times [1 + (15/12)]\} + 2 \times 12 \\
&= 609 \\
\text{Number of entities accessed} &= 4N_e + 8N_r \\
&= 4 \times 12 + 8 \times 15 \\
&= 168 \\
\text{Number of output fields} &= \{N_a \times [1 + (N_r/N_e)]\} + 3N_e \\
&= \{130 \times [1 + (15/12)]\} + 3 \times 12 \\
&= 329 \\
\text{Unadjusted function points} &= 0.58 \times 609 + 1.66 \times 168 + 0.26 \times 329 \\
&= 718
\end{aligned}
$$

B.5 COMMENTS ON RESULTS

There is only a fairly small difference (less than 15%) between the size calculation based on the UFP matrix and that obtained by assessing each logical transaction. This can probably be adequately resolved by the following observations:

- The timetable transactions were assessed as complex, and yet were assessed as only having a small number of fields and entities.
- Similarly, the transactions for both clinic and surgery were assessed as complex and yet they too only were assessed as having a small number of fields and entities.

The difference between the function-based approach and the data-based approach is much larger, the data-based approach giving a result around 75% larger than the function-based approach. This size of discrepancy should trigger an evaluation of both estimates in order to try to reconcile the differences. Some of the factors that have contributed in this case are:

- When compiling the list of transactions for the function-based approach, no transactions were provided to maintain the doctor entity or the patient type entity.
- The function-based approach only provides for 5 delete transactions and yet there are 12 entities.
- The function-based approach only allows emergency home visits and emergency appointments to be created; it does not apparently allow for their deletion, alteration or even being inquired upon.

There are other differences; the ones listed would, however, explain a substantial portion of the difference. Having understood the difference, you are in a position to decide which view is correct. If the data-based view was held to be more correct then it would be necessary to revisit the list of transactions for the function-based approach, correct them and rework the calculations.

These discrepancies between results, although contrived for the purpose of illustration here, can and do arise for legitimate reasons on real projects. It is quite in order to build systems in which some information will never be altered or deleted, so care must be taken while considering discrepancies. However, it is equally possible that the discrepancy has arisen because of faulty analysis, and in these circumstances the ability to compare two separately derived estimates can be invaluable.

APPENDIX C: SAMPLE SOLUTION FOR CHAPTER 4 CASE STUDY

C.1 LIST OF CLASSIFIED TRANSACTIONS

The following three worksheets (Figs C.1, C.2 and C.3) show

- Transactions with named inputs, entities and outputs identified
- A final function point count for the administration facilities
- Sizing for each transaction

As with the other case studies, producing the same result as the authors on the first attempt is not the aim. The important thing is to understand the differences between your answer and the sample solution.

If you find that your answer differs because of your approach to counting then please re-read the relevant portion of Chapter 4. If your answer is different due to transcription or arithmetic errors then move on to Chapter 5 – but be more careful next time!

Transaction component identification worksheet	
System	Patient contact system – Administration facilities
Phase	Logical system design
Date	28 April 1994
Assessor	S. Treble/N. Douglas

Transaction id	Inputs	Entities	Outputs
New patient	New patient details	Patient Patient type User User privs	New patient ack. New patient card
Change to patient	Changed patient details	Patient Patient type User User privs	Changed patient ack. Changed patient card
Patient enquiry	Request for patient details	Patient Patient type	Patient details
Patient leaves	Delete patient request	Patient User User privs Appt slot	Deleted patient ack.
New surgery type	New surgery type	Surgery format	New surgery type ack.
Change to surgery type	Changed surgery type	Surgery format	Changed surgery type ack.
Surgery type enquiry	Request for surgery	Surgery format	Surgery type details
Surgery type redundant	Delete surgery type	Surgery format Surgery	Deleted surgery type ack.
New clinic type	New clinic type	Clinic format	New clinic type ack.
Change to clinic type	Changed clinic type	Clinic format	Changed clinic type ack.
Clinic type enquiry	Request for clinic	Clinic format	Clinic type details
Clinic type redundant	Delete clinic type	Clinic format Clinic	Deleted clinic type ack.
Schedule a clinic	Add a clinic	Clinic Clinic format Timetabled event	New clinic response
Schedule a surgery	Add a surgery	Surgery Surgery format Timetabled event	New surgery ack.
Scheduled clinic changed	Change a clinic	Clinic Clinic format Timetabled event	Change a clinic ack.
Scheduled surgery changed	Change a surgery	Surgery Surgery format Timetabled event	Changed surgery ack.
Scheduled clinic enquiry	Request for clinic details	Clinic Timetabled event	Scheduled clinic details
Scheduled surgery enquiry	Request for surgery details	Surgery Timetabled event	Scheduled surgery details
Clinic cancelled	Cancel a clinic	Clinic Timetabled event Appointment slot	Cancelled clinic ack.
Surgery cancelled	Cancel surgery req.	Surgery Timetabled event Appointment slot	Cancelled surgery ack.
Produce day's timetable	Req. for day's timetable	Timetabled event	Timetables

Figure C.1 Transaction component identification worksheet.

Transaction counting worksheet			
System	Patient contact system – Administration facilities		
Phase	Logical system design		
Date	28 April 1994		
Assessor	S. Treble/N. Douglas		

Transaction id	**Inputs**	**Entities**	**Outputs**
New patient	7	3	13
Change to patient	6	3	13
Patient enquiry	1	2	8
Patient leaves	1	3	4
New surgery type	5	1	5
Change to surgery type	4	1	5
Surgery type enquiry	1	1	3
Surgery type redundant	1	2	3
New clinic type	5	1	6
Change to clinic type	7	1	6
Clinic type enquiry	3	1	7
Clinic type redundant	1	2	3
Schedule a clinic	5	3	7
Schedule a surgery	5	3	7
Scheduled clinic changed	6	3	6
Scheduled surgery changed	6	3	6
Scheduled clinic enquiry	3	2	7
Scheduled surgery enquiry	3	2	6
Clinic cancelled	3	3	3
Surgery cancelled	2	3	3
Produce day's timetable	1	1	9
Totals	76	44	130

Figure C.2 Transaction counting worksheet.

System sizing worksheet			
System	Patient contact system – Administration facilities		
Phase	Logical system design		
Date	28 April 1994		
Assessor	S. Treble/N. Douglas		

	Inputs	**Entities**	**Outputs**
Total transaction components	76	44	130
× Weighting	0.58	1.66	0.26
giving UFP	44.08	73.04	33.8
Total UFP			150.9

Figure C.3 System sizing worksheet.

APPENDIX D: SAMPLE SOLUTION FOR CHAPTER 5 CASE STUDY

Those of you who have worked through the other case studies can skip the next two paragraphs. The rest read on . . .

As with the other case studies, producing the same result as the authors on the first attempt is not the aim. The important thing is to understand the differences between your answer and the sample solution.

If you find that your answer differs because of your approach to counting then please re-read the relevant portion of Chapter 5. If your answer is different due to transcription or arithmetic errors then move on to Chapter 6 – but be more careful next time!

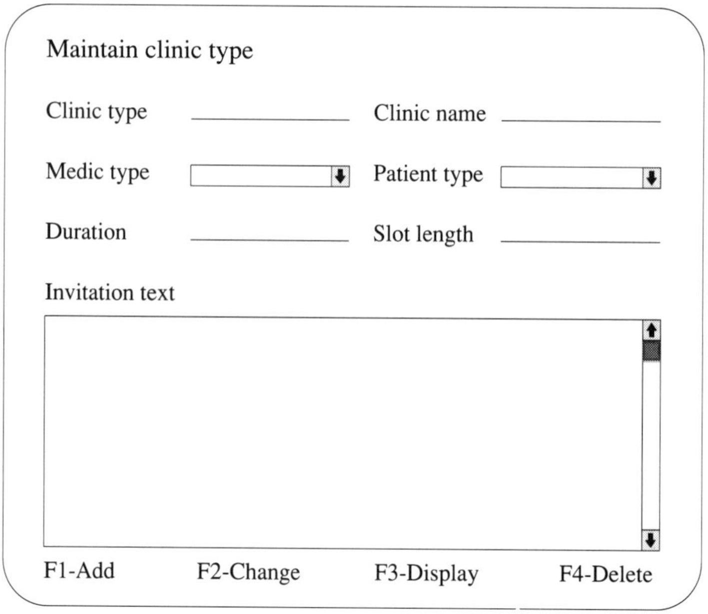

Maintain clinic type	
Clinic type _____	Clinic name _____
Medic type [⬇]	Patient type [⬇]
Duration _____	Slot length _____
Invitation text	

F1-Add   F2-Change   F3-Display   F4-Delete

Figure D.1 Maintain clinic type.

Exercise 1: Clinic maintenance screen

This screen (Fig. D.1) offers four logical transactions:

- Add clinic type
- Change (i.e. amend) details of a clinic type
- Display details of a clinic type
- Delete a clinic type

These transactions are identified and sized in Tables D.1 and D.2.

Table D.1 Transaction identification

Transaction	Inputs	Entities referenced	Outputs
Add clinic type	Clinic type, Clinic name, Medic. type description, Patient type description, Duration, Slot length, Invitation text	Clinic format, Patient type, Medic. type	Success/failure message
Change clinic type	Clinic type, Clinic name, Medic. type description, Patient type description, Duration, Slot length, Invitation text	Clinic format, Patient type, Medic. type	Success/failure message
Display clinic type	Clinic type	Clinic format, Patient type, Medic. type	Clinic name, Medic. type, Patient type, Duration, Slot length, Invitation text
Delete clinic type	Clinic type	Clinic format	Success/failure message

Table D.2 Transaction sizes

Transaction	Inputs	Entities referenced	Outputs	UFP
Add clinic type	7	2	1	7.64
Change clinic type	7	2	1	7.64
Display clinic type	1	2	6	5.46
Delete clinic type	1	1	1	2.50

Exercise 2: Add patient

The following screens (Fig. D.2) combine to form a single add patient logical transaction. The fact that the transaction is split over two screens does not affect the number of transactions.

The sizing for the logical transaction is shown in Table D.3

The facility to page back and forward between the two screens (i.e. Alt-N and Alt-P) is not included in the count since it has been provided to overcome technology limitations. This sort of facility falls into the same category as menus: were the physical display large enough to accommodate the entire transaction then the facility would not have been provided – it does not form part of the business processing.

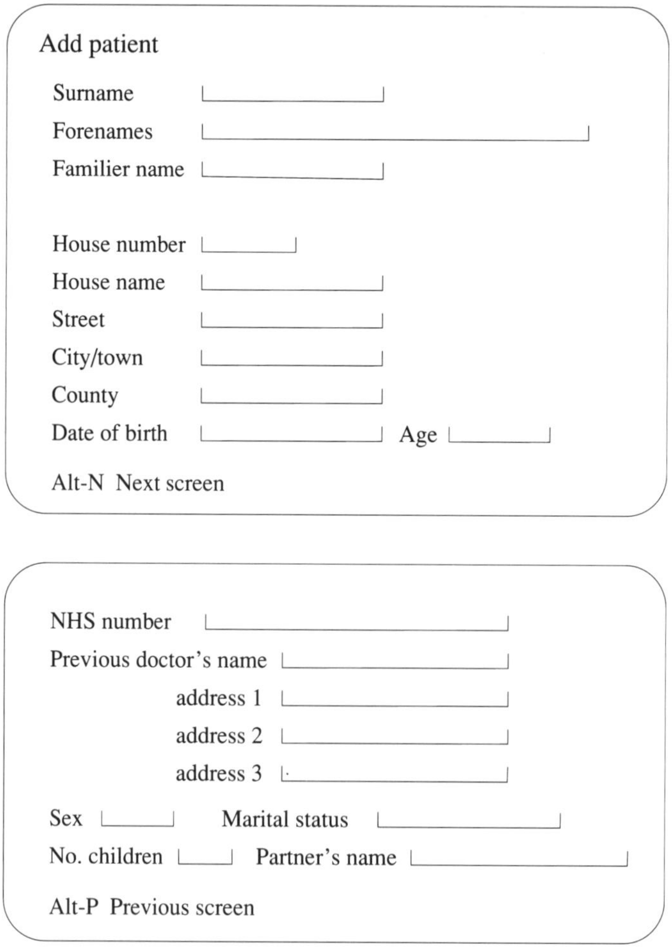

Add patient

Surname

Forenames

Familier name

House number

House name

Street

City/town

County

Date of birth   Age

Alt-N Next screen

NHS number

Previous doctor's name

address 1

address 2

address 3

Sex   Marital status

No. children   Partner's name

Alt-P Previous screen

Figure D.2 Add patient screens.

Table D.3 Sizing

Inputs	Entities referenced	Outputs	UFP
Surname, Forename, Familier name, House number, House name, Street, City/town, County, Date of birth, Age, NHS number, Previous doctor's name, Address (lines 1 to 3), Sex, Marital status, Number of children, Partner's name	Patient	Success/failure message	
17	1	1	11.78

Finally, the fact that fields exist on screen which do not appear in the logical system design (see case study Chapter 4) does not alter the fact that they are included in the count in the same way as other fields. The tricky bit is to decide which entity to assign them to. In this case we have assumed that they all belong to the patient entity. The assumption was made for the sake of simplicity; there are good arguments for storing address and previous doctor information as separate entities, so if your answer differs for that sort of reason then do not worry.

Exercise 3: Clinic report

Transactions which are split over time for technology reasons are still counted as only one logical transaction. In this case, the transaction has been split into separate on-line and batch transactions to avoid overloading the central database. Even if there was a user requirement stating that normal business transactions must have a certain response time, and in this case the report had been split between on-line and batch in order to allow normal business transactions to meet the requirement, that would not change the fact that this is still only one logical transaction.

An example of a situation where a split between on-line and batch may count as two logical transactions would be where the *user* required all output to be generated at once. For instance, the postal service may offer incentives for businesses that could sort their mail by postcode. In this instance, it may be that letters are keyed in during the day and automatically sorted, printed and put in envelopes overnight. Clearly here is a logical transaction (i.e. produce a letter) that is split over time for business reasons.

Fig. D.3 shows the report on clinic type by practitioner. The transaction is sized as shown in Table D.4.

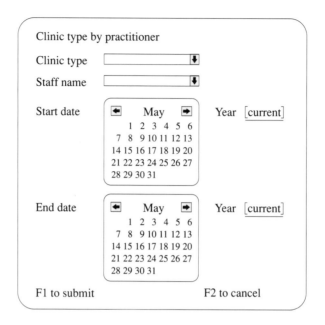

Figure D.3 Report on clinic type by practitioner.

Table D.4 Transaction sizing

Inputs	Entities referenced	Outputs	UFP
Clinic name, Staff name, Start day, Start month, Start year, End day, End month, End year	Clinic, Clinic format, Medical staff	Clinic type, Date, Number of patients, Clinic name	
8	3	4	10.66

APPENDIX E: SAMPLE SOLUTION FOR CHAPTER 6 CASE STUDY

Those of you who have worked through the other case studies, can skip the next two paragraphs. The rest read on . . .

As with the other case studies, producing the same result as the authors on the first attempt is not the aim. The important thing is to understand the differences between your answer and the sample solution.

If you find that your answer differs because of your approach to counting then please re-read the relevant portion of Chapter 6. If your answer is different due to transcription or arithmetic errors then move on to Chapter 7 – but be more careful next time!

Exercise 1: Add patient screen enhancement

The enhancement requested in Exercise 1 will clearly affect more than just the add patient screen. However, we have been asked to estimate the impact on the add patient screen (Fig. E.1). From Appendix D we know that only one logical transaction uses this screen.

In order to sort letters to patients in order of postcode, it is necessary to record the postcode of each patient. An additional field is therefore required, and in this system it is the patient entity that needs to be altered to store the postcode. Therefore the change in size is as shown in Table E.1.

Note that we have counted 1 against entities referenced to reflect the fact that an entity required alteration. This does not mean that there is an additional entity referenced by the transaction: it merely sizes the amount of work to be done in the enhancement. No outputs were counted, since none have been altered.

Table E.1 Change in transaction size

Inputs	Entities referenced	Outputs	UFP
1	1	0	2.24

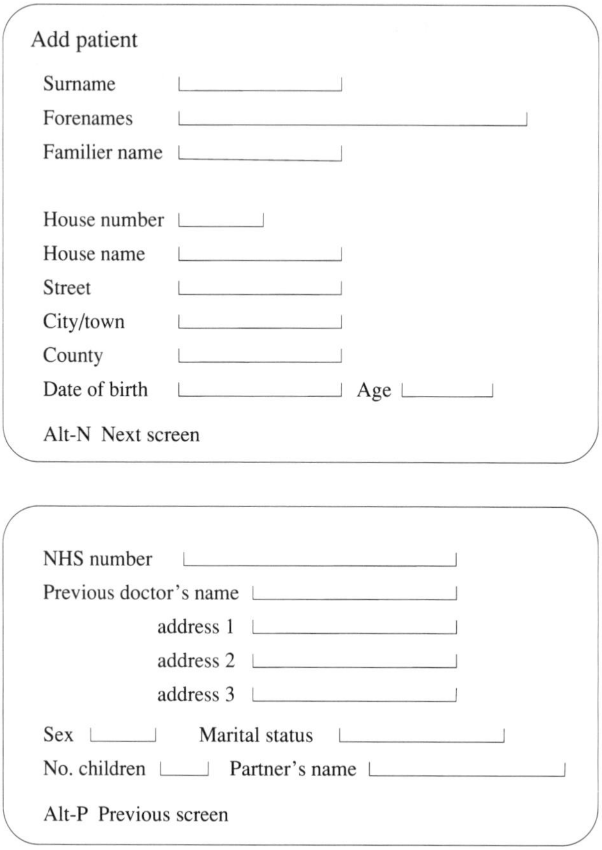

Add patient

    Surname _____

    Forenames _____

    Familier name _____

    House number _____

    House name _____

    Street _____

    City/town _____

    County _____

    Date of birth _____ Age _____

    Alt-N Next screen

    NHS number _____

    Previous doctor's name _____

    address 1 _____

    address 2 _____

    address 3 _____

    Sex _____ Marital status _____

    No. children _____ Partner's name _____

    Alt-P Previous screen

Figure E.1 Add patient screens.

The amended transaction is sized as shown in Table E.2.

Table E.2 Final transaction size

Inputs	Entities referenced	Outputs	UFP
Surname, Forename, Familier name, House number, House name, Street, City/town, County, Postcode, Date of birth, Age, NHS number, Previous doctor's name, Address (lines 1 to 3), Sex, Marital status, Number of children, Partner's name	Patient	Success/failure message	
18	1	1	12.36

Exercise 2: Add patient screen enhancement

Figure E.1 shows the original add patient screen. This change is simple: there is one field to be removed from the screen. However, now that the business no longer requires the age field to be entered, there is an argument that says that it should not be stored on the system. The arguments surrounding this can become quite complex but we shall take the view that the field indicates the age of patients when they joined the practice and shall therefore leave it on the database (the field being calculated and stored by the system when new patients are entered).

Thus the change is one input field deleted and an unadjusted function point count of −0.58. The recalculated size is shown in Table E.3.

Table E.3 Final transaction size

Inputs	Entities referenced	Outputs	UFP
Surname, Forename, Familier name, House number, House name, Street, City/town, County, Date of birth, NHS number, Previous doctor's name, Address (lines 1 to 3), Sex, Marital status, Number of children, Partner's name	Patient	Success/failure message	
16	1	1	11.2

Exercise 3: Enhancements to the clinic type by practitioner report

The first change required is to sort the report (Fig. E.2) into alphabetical order by practitioner. This has no impact on the function point size since the sequence in which the output is presented has no impact on the function point count. From the viewpoint of function points, we are interested solely in the field types comprising an output record and not in the sequence in which output records are produced.

The optional limit to show only those clinics where the clinic time represents more than 10% of the actual weekly workload is a measurable change. An input field is required to control the optional limit and a change to the processing is required but there are no changes to the output fields (despite the fact that fewer records are printed).

The processing change means that a new entity is referenced, *timetabled event*, in order to find out the workload of the practitioner. The clinic and medical staff entities will be processed differently in order to calculate the effort spent on each clinic type. Thus the size of the change is as shown in Table E.4.

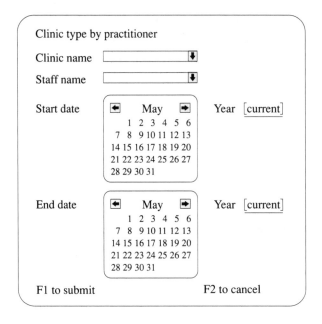

Figure E.2 Report on clinic type by practitioner.

Table E.4 Change in transaction size

Inputs	Entities referenced	Outputs	UFP
Limit Y/N	Clinic, Medical staff, Timetabled event		
1	3	0	5.56

Table E.5 shows the size of the transaction after the change.

Table E.5 Final transaction size

Inputs	Entities referenced	Outputs	UFP
Clinic name, Staff name, Start day, Start month, Start year, End day, End month, End year, Limit Y/N	Clinic, Clinic format, Medical staff, Timetabled event	Clinic type, Date, Number of patients, Clinic name, Practitioner	
9	4	5	13.16

Exercise 4: Clinic type by practitioner for the receptionist

Chapter 2 states that a logical transaction is '. . . triggered by a unique business event . . .'. The business event of the practice manager requiring to balance the workload of the practice across practitioners is different from the business event of the receptionist identifying patients who should attend clinics.

In this case, however, the same report can be used for each. Since the business events are different, there must be two logical transactions being provided by the one report: one for the practice manager and one for the receptionist. Therefore the impact on system size is quite simple; the logical transaction is counted again as shown in Table E.6.

Table E.6 Final transaction size

Inputs	Entities referenced	Outputs	UFP
Clinic name, Staff name, Start day, Start month, Start year, End day, End month, End year	Clinic, Clinic format, Medical staff, Timetabled event	Clinic type, Date, Number of patients, Clinic name, Practitioner	
8	4	5	12.58

APPENDIX F: SAMPLE SOLUTION FOR CHAPTER 7 CASE STUDY

F.1 ESTIMATE FOR THE PATIENT ADMINISTRATION SYSTEM

1. Identify and size the logical transactions

See Appendix B, Section 3.

2. Calculate the normative project effort and duration

We are assuming the project is all to be done in a 3GL and that the industry average figures are applicable.

From Appendix B, the project size is 398 UFP. The TCA we were given was 0.85, so:

$$\text{FPI} = 398 \times 0.85 = 338$$

Looking up the industry average productivity gives a value of 0.12 function points per work hour. This translates to a normative project effort of:

$$\text{Effort} = 338/0.12 = 2817 \text{ hours}$$

The delivery rate is:

$$\text{Delivery} = 0.45 \times \text{square root } (338) = 8.27 \text{ function points/week}$$

and thus the elapsed time is:

$$\text{Duration} = 338/8.27 = 41 \text{ weeks}$$

3. Allocate effort and duration to the phases of the project

Using the industry standard model:

Phase	Effort	Elapsed time
Analysis	620	15
Design	423	6
Code	1295	10
Test	338	6
Install	141	4

4. Adjust the effort and duration to account for project environmental factors

We have been told to increase the analysis effort by 50 hours to account for a poorly documented existing system:

Phase	Effort	Elapsed time
Analysis	670	15
Design	423	6
Code	1295	10
Test	338	6
Install	141	4

5. Consider project deadlines and adjust the effort and schedule accordingly

The project must complete within 35 weeks, and our estimate is 41 weeks. Thus we have a schedule compression factor of:

$$SCF = 35/41 = 0.85$$

This must be applied to each phase in order to adjust the effort. The duration of each phase must also be adjusted to account for the deadline.

Phase	Effort	Elapsed time
Analysis	788	12
Design	498	5
Code	1524	9
Test	398	5
Install	166	4

6. Calculate headcount by phase

Assuming 65% utilization over a 35 hour week:

$$\text{Headcount} = 0.044 \times \text{work hours/elapsed weeks}$$

Thus for our example:

Phase	Headcount	Effort	Elapsed time
Analysis	2.89	788	12
Design	4.38	498	5
Code	7.45	1524	9
Test	3.50	398	5
Install	1.83	166	4

7. Revise headcount in line with known staffing constraints

No staff constraints were specified, so we can either stop now or round the headcount. For the example, we shall round the headcount up to the nearest half person.

The formulae to apply to each phase are :

$$RAF = \text{root(rounded headcount)/root(unrounded headcount)}$$
$$\text{New effort} = \text{old effort} \times RAF$$
$$\text{New duration} = \text{old duration}/RAF$$

Phase	Headcount	Effort	Elapsed time
Analysis	3	803	12
Design	4.5	505	5
Code	7.5	1529	9
Test	3.5	398	5
Install	2	174	4

The total project effort = 3409, and duration is 35 weeks. The implied productivity is 338/3409 = 0.10 function points per work hour at a delivery of 338/35 = 9.66 function points per elapsed week.

Small differences between the above solution and the reader's solution may arise due to rounding errors.

F.2 CONCLUSION

The above is an example of applying the technique to a project which the reader will be familiar with from their earlier study. This should give some confidence both in applying the technique and in the results obtained.

REFERENCES

DeMarco, T. (1982). *Controlling Software Projects*, Prentice Hall, New Jersey.
Fenton, N. (1991). *Software Metrics: a Rigorous Approach*, Chapman & Hall, London.
Goodman, P. (1994). *Practical Implementation of Software Metrics*, McGraw-Hill, London.
Symons, C. R. (1991). *Software Sizing and Estimating: MKII Function Point Analysis*, John Wiley & Sons, Chichester.

INDEX

Abend type defects, 109
Advice and assistance, 108–9
Albrecht, Alan, 3, 23
Algorithmic techniques, 139
Analysis project phase, 52
Audit, 24, 121

Batch:
  case study, 104, 171
  estimating, 44, 141, 148
  programs, 97–8
  reports, 86
  sizing, approach, 86, 96, 97–8, 103
Bought-in packages, how to count, 102

Calibration, 147–51
CASE tools, 9, 54
Changes (*see* Enhancements)
Conversation table in place of data flow
    diagrams, 61
Counting software tools, how to, 102
CRUD (Create, Reference, Update, Delete)
    matrix, 24, 59, 63

Data analysis, project activity 59
Data dictionary, using for FPA, 53, 63–4
Data flow diagrams (DFD), 16, 30–1, 47, 53,
    55–7
  alternatives to, 60
  conversation table in place of, 61
  marking logical transactions on, 50–1
  not available, 60
Data and function models, non-
    matching, 72–3
Data store/entity cross-reference matrix, 63
Defects:
  abend, 109
  as part of performance measurement, 9
  as part of quality measurement, 134

categorization, 134
functional, 109
Delivery:
  definition, 130
  estimation, 141–3
  measurement, 1, 133
Development process, definition, 130, 131
Documentation (useful):
  existing systems, 85
  inadequate for counting, 55, 60–1
  logical design, 53–4
  potential source for counting, 23, 28–9,
    50–4, 72
  recording counts, 50, 121

Elementary processes, 55
Enhancements, 110–20
  case study, 123–5, 173–7
  definition, 107, 110
  measures appropriate for, 110–11
  sizing, 111–12
  worked examples, 112–20
Entity/datastore cross references, 54
Entity/process models, 54
Entity(ies):
  case study model, 48
  common documents, 54
  identification, 61–3
  primary, 18, 19, 65
  role in function point analysis, 18–19
  system, 18, 19, 65
  types of, 19, 65
  worked example model, 34
Environment categories, 149
Event/entity cross-reference matrix, 53, 61,
    72
  entities identified from, 63
  not available, 63

Related titles are available in McGraw-Hill's International Software Quality Assurance Series